Voices from Labour's Past

March - 2015.

To Christobel with love.
My Mother - Jess Nally. pages 57-80

Voices from
Labour's Past

Ordinary People Extraordinary Lives

DAVID CLARK

LENSDEN PUBLISHING

Lensden Publishing
© David Clark
Published 2015

ISBN: 978-0-9575891-1-7

Front Cover:
Detail from Labour Party poster 1931

Printed by MTP Media, Beezon Fields, Kendal, Cumbria, LA9 6BL

Contents

Preface and Acknowledgements

The Labour Party is a little over a hundred years old. I have been a member of the Party for more than half a century and thus for half of its existence. When I joined I had the pleasure and privilege of working alongside people who had been Party members almost since its inception. The early forgotten Labour pioneers who feature in this book made considerable sacrifices as they helped Labour develop into a successful political force.

The political world in which they began their task is unrecognisable to us living today. These pioneers made history. But the history they made was not the type of history that was taught in their day. History has too often been about kings and queens and certainly not about the lives of ordinary men and women. Although on occasions history has been stretched to include Labour and trade union leaders, it has neglected the rank and file.

Indeed it is only in the last forty or so years that with the advent of oral history and the availability of archival material, interest in the past lives of ordinary people has become acceptable.

In the 1960s and 1970s, I met many of these early pioneers and increasingly felt that their stories ought to be told. I began to document their lives and record their experiences. It wasn't the easiest of tasks for, whilst they might trust me, they were suspicious of the cumbersome recording equipment of the day which seemed to fill their living rooms. Nevertheless I managed to interview over thirty early activists. These interviews provide a rich reservoir for anyone wishing to understand how Labour became one of the two principal political parties in Britain. Ordinary men and women, they lived extraordinary lives.

The eight interviewees I have selected for the book have much to tell us about how and why Labour became the political force that it did.

For these pioneers the years of, and surrounding, World War I were critical in their political lives. One striking feature of the women's life stories is the criticality of the War to the suffrage movement. As the War began, so many radical young women who felt the injustice of being deprived of the vote, began to see the wider injustices of society. This was especially so when Mrs Pankhurst suspended the suffrage campaign in 1914 and took an unquestioning patriotic line. Thus during the war many young, often middle-class women, switched their energies to the Independent Labour Party, with its anti-war leadership. Their influence was transferred to the Labour Party and remained strong well into the second half of the twentieth century. They brought many organisational skills and contacts with them and laid the ground work for an unprecedented emancipation effort which allowed tens of thousands of working women to develop their skills and play a part in political life.

What is equally striking is the effect of World War I on the political balance in Britain. Both the Liberal and Labour parties were split by the war. The result however, was that the Liberals never recovered whilst Labour prospered. In the General Election of December 1910, Labour's vote was a mere 376,581 but by 1918 this had increased to 2,385,472. At the following election of 1922, its vote increased hugely to 4,076,665 and 142 MPs. Then in 1923, the vote increased yet again and Labour managed to form a minority Government with the Party gaining added credibility as its MPs became Ministers of the Crown.

A further feature often overlooked was the effect of the Labour Party's apparently, purely organisational reforms in 1918 by Arthur Henderson. The first of his two crucial reforms allowed men and women to become members as individuals for the first time and the second provided formal recognition for women to have their rights guaranteed within the Party's structure. These changes struck a chord with those men and women who were given the vote for the first time in 1918. They also permitted an alternative to the ILP for those who wished to play a role in the Labour Party but were not members of a trade union or socialist society. As Jowitt and Laybourn point out in Bradford for example, many ILP members who were not anti-war found an avenue as individual members of the Labour Party through which to pursue their left-wing political objectives. In that city, as elsewhere, it began the gradual demise of the ILP and accompanied the growth of membership, especially among women, in the Labour Party.

However all eight of the individuals in this book were against the war. This was unusual even in the Labour movement. The overwhelming number of the Party's supporters took a patriotic line with some of its MPs serving as ministers in the war-time government. Coincidentally, four out of the five men were conscientious objectors including one who was among a very small number of 'absolutists', whilst the fifth, although opposed to the war, was excused military service as he was doing work of national importance.

Even in the ILP, whose leaders were almost all anti-war, the majority of members supported the war. Indeed a survey of members of the extremely active Bradford branch found that before conscription in 1916, out of 461 eligible for service, 237 had volunteered for service whilst a further 207 were on work of national importance. In 1918 only 48 were either COs or on work of national importance out of 492 eligible for service. To further emphasise the point, the miners at Westerhope Colliery on Tyneside, refused to work alongside fellow miner, Will Lewcock (Chapter 7), because he was against the conflict and he had to move away. However, as the war progressed, and especially after conscription was introduced in 1916, there was some movement of opinion in favour of a negotiated peace.

One aspect of writing this book from the perspective of a politician has been my appreciation that the individuals saw themselves as 'nothing out of the ordinary'. In fact in some cases their obscurity has been evidenced by the difficulties in finding any surviving photographs. Few if any photographs remain, most have been lost or destroyed. I am grateful for those who have helped me locate those used in the book.

I owe a debt of gratitude to the University of Huddersfield which encouraged me to begin this research forty years ago and have continued with their support. In particular Professor Brendan Evans and Professor Keith Laybourn have been towers of strength throughout.

Archivists and librarians throughout the country have been of great assistance. In particular, the staff of the Cumbria Archives Centres of Cumbria County Council have continually provided me with a first class service and I am especially indebted to Catherine Clark at Whitehaven and Peter Eyre at Kendal. Furthermore, as always the staff of the

House of Lords' Library have dealt with my obscure queries with patience and tolerance.

Many individuals have helped me over the years with the research but a number stand out. Win Wheable-Archer has discussed her mother's experiences in great detail and allowed me to quote from her splendid autobiography. Margaret Firth has been most accommodating in providing additional information on her uncle, Gladstone Mathers. Maureen Calcott very kindly supplied me with the photograph of Margaret Gibb and further details of her life. Mike Shaw was generous, as always in giving me the benefit over the years of his unrivalled local knowledge of Colne Valley. Trevor and Wendy Sanderson have gone beyond the bounds of friendship in helping with their knowledge of John Beaumont whilst Baroness Taylor of Bolton made available her research on early activists of the Holme Valley. Cyril Pearce kindly provided me with details from his extensive records of conscientious objectors. Professor Julia Brannen has given me the benefit of her valuable experience of using oral history. Julie Ward has proved herself to be a first-rate researcher, giving generously of her time and energy and has spent hours trawling through newspapers and documents not to mention driving miles to talk to relatives of the early pioneers.

Finally, I cannot praise my publisher, Rev. Dr Leonard Smith, highly enough. He is a noted Labour historian and has given me wise advice in the preparation of this book. He has shown patience, understanding and kindness for which I am most grateful.

But it is for all those early Labour Party activists that I reserve my greatest thanks. They left me in awe with the appreciation of their absolute dedication to build a better society. They succeeded and all rightly felt their sacrifices had been worthwhile. Each of them knew, they left Britain a better society than the one in which they were born in the late nineteenth century. There can hardly be a better epitaph.

I

WILLIAM WATSON
1887-1987

Few people have travelled to West Cumberland. Encompassing a large part of the English Lake District National Park, it includes some of the most beautiful landscapes in Britain, but also an industrial belt in that tract of land between the mountains and the Irish Sea. Underlying this area are rich deposits of coal, iron-ore and limestone, all the essential components for an iron and steel industry. In the Victorian period the industry prospered but following the temporary fillip created by the demands for steel in World War I, industrial decline occurred rapidly and the most appalling economic and social conditions ensued.

The problem became so acute that in the 1930s, the Government were forced to investigate. The Chancellor of the Duchy of Lancaster, the Rt Hon. J C C Davidson, began his report by summarising the situation,

> Scattered in the valleys and on the foothills that lead down to the sea are villages where men have no work whatsoever. The local mine has closed never to re-open, and there is no alternative occupation. To appreciate the problem of West Cumberland, two elementary facts must be recognised; the first, that it is a lovely county, to which its inhabitants are most deeply attached; and the second, that it is geographically remote, hidden from the rest of the country by a high range of hills.

That official Government Report of 1934 found unemployment levels in the area often in excess of 50 per cent and in the Cleator Moor Employment Exchange Area, where William Watson lived, it reached 65.8 per cent in December 1932. The township of Frizington, 'which has perhaps more cause than any other town or village in Cumberland to be termed "derelict" with "practically no work available in the Frizington and Arlecdon portions of the area".' (Cmd 4728, 1934 pp.10-13).

More graphically, a Manchester University Study of two years previously said of Frizington, 'the conditions…almost beggar description for this town is almost completely without employment of any kind, and without hope of it in the future' (Jewkes, 1933 p.10). This was the community, in which William Watson lived as a child, went to school, began his working life and in time became the chair of the local council.

William Watson (still alert) in his nineties

William Watson was born on the 28 August 1887 in the village of Brigham near Cockermouth. His father, Thomas, was a quarryman, as his father had been before him. As was often the case in those years, the Watsons moved in with the wife's parents and the 1891 Census shows that six adults and four children were living in the same house at 43 The Village.

Soon after this, Thomas got a job in a quarry a few miles to the south in Rowrah in the township of Arlecdon and Frizington. The family grew up there with William having five brothers and two sisters. Thomas was a Methodist and Liberal and was obviously conscientious and able, for he was eventually made the manager of the Rowrah Hall Quarry. Although this meant a higher wage it was not without worries as William explained many years later.

> I remember he was on a contract basis and there was a lot of blasting involved and the cost of explosives went up high. He was using a great lot of explosives and at the month end, he found he was in a lot of debt and it worried him greatly. He worked hard, he applied his best endeavours and his best knowledge to his work and I remember it was a great worry to him. While the men were poorly paid so were the management. They were poorly paid. I remember him saying 'there is nothing in the world that would please me so much as for someone to come along and say that they would pay my explosive bill for last month'. But it didn't happen.

Of course when he was very young these worries were of little concern to William who had a very happy childhood in this rural industrial village. He recalled,

> The first thing I remember of my childhood, I would be less than four, I'd be three and a half. My mother sent me to school and I didn't land at school. It was springtime, and me and a pal, who later turned out to be the brother of Lady Adams (later the wife of Lord Adams of Ennerdale) was blamed too. We went bird-nesting. We got corrected when we went home and mother found out we hadn't been to school.

William's description of those times is supplemented in an unpublished biography of Jack Adams, who became a Labour Peer and who grew up alongside William Watson, by a West Cumberland journalist, Frank Carruthers. It graphically catches those halcyon days of schoolchildren growing up in the area in spite of the grinding poverty, in which they lived:

We all wore clothes which had been handed down from older brothers. Old clothes, patched perhaps but never with holes. Carefully kept and carefully mended but always subject to violent treatment in the schoolyard and on expeditions down to Dub Beck where we caught minnows.

Paddling in Dub Beck, ratching along the hedgerows for black-berries which were absolutely necessary if the local families were to have some jam for their bread. Going nutting for hazel nuts and when time allowed especially in the summer holidays, long excursions up on Knockburton Fell for bilberries, always a great delicacy. We returned blue-lipped and full of iron that the bilber-ries were supposed to inject into the system.

School was not very much fun. It was a daily grind of reading, writing and arithmetic. Everyone wore clogs, few people even owned shoes. Men wore their pit clogs to work and kept highly polished and brassy clogs with duck nebs for their Sunday best. Women wore clogs about the house and often all the time and children wore clogs to school. The whole district echoed day and night to the clatter of caulkered clogs as children pattered to school and men clumped to work, and women pottered about their house. Clogs hardly ever wore out. All they required was an occasional set of iron caulkers. The average man about the house could put these on himself. The cast iron last was as much part of the household furniture as the teapot.

Life was lived in the villages. Few could afford to travel, even to the nearest towns and children grew up into man - and woman-hood - in Arlecdon without ever seeing Whitehaven, some even without visiting Cleator Moor where there was a weekly market. The village provided all the needs of work and food and clothing for there was always a village dressmaker, always a travelling man coming round with a horse and trap.

Children grew up sturdily on a diet of bread, potatoes and porridge and on broth, made in a setpot in the washhouse, of leeks
and greens and a sheep's head or a ham shank. On a miner's wage
of three or four shillings there was nothing for anything but the
bare necessities of life. When children came in from school, a
wad of bread with or without jam was all they expected or
got. If they were lucky they had meat on Sundays (Carruthers,
unpublished document, nd).

The school in question was the local one in Arlecdon, just a few minutes' walk from William's home. All in all, he enjoyed the school where
he stayed until leaving in 1900 at the age of thirteen. Not surprisingly, he
went to work under his father in the quarry, a mere ten minutes walk
from the family home in Arlecdon Park Road. He spent his adolescence
working there and doing what teenagers in Edwardian Britain did. There
was a very active football club in the village and of course there were the
local girls to chase, when he met Sarah Johnston and began courting her.
It is worthy of note in view of his later activities, he had no interest in
political or trade union matters during these years.

West Cumberland had experienced an industrial boom in the last quarter of the nineteenth century but then decline had really set in. A tradition developed for young men from the area to emigrate to Australia,
Canada or New Zealand in search of work and a better life. If they found
success they often would send for their families or sweethearts. As hap-
pens in most emigrations, the migrants usually travelled to destinations
where other people from their home districts had previously settled.

After a few years at the quarry, the economy locally became even further depressed and in 1909, a local family, known to William through the
chapel, returned on a visit from Canada and spoke enthusiastically about
their adopted country.

Almost seventy years later, he recalled thinking about emigrating to
Canada,

Well things were very bad here, very bad indeed. So I began
thinking of trying my luck in Canada. The Government over
there sent people back to Britain to persuade young people to

emigrate. I remember the first people that went out to Vancouver, the Wilkinsons of Prospect, came over here recruiting. He was a minister of mining, I think, of the Canadian Government and they wanted men to develop that industry and they came over here recruiting.

William discussed it with Sarah and decided to start saving up for the fare to travel to Canada which was not easy on the wages of a young quarryman. At the age of twenty-three in 1910, the young Cumbrian left his native Arlecdon to try his luck in Canada. His ship left Liverpool and 'it was raining when I left and when I came back six years later it was still raining!' The sea voyage terminated in Halifax, Nova Scotia and from there the long journey continued by rail. He stopped off at Moose Jaw, Saskatchewan where he found employment in the offices of the Canadian Pacific Railway Company. But this was frontier territory and the conditions were extremely primitive. Even the deprivations of industrial West Cumberland had not prepared the young migrant for this, 'there was no sanitation and very little water supply'. To make matters worse, whilst he was there, a typhoid epidemic broke out and William was taken severely ill.

Fortunately, as he described later,

> Mrs Watson's brother and her sister's husband came over from England with a view of settling in Canada just as I had done. They saw me at Moose Jaw and I had been there three months and I'd failed so much in health in that time, they were afraid for me, actually afraid for me. They thought if I stayed there much longer I was going to die. And they were probably right, I probably would have. So I decided to go to Vancouver. I had relatives in Vancouver; seven cousins. While we had no jobs to go to, I knew it would be alright for we would be put up with some of my cousins. I got a job digging trenches in that city to put sewers in and water supplies and this sort of thing. It was a new town and I worked in that for a while and then in the course of time that job finished. Then the mines were the only things left so I went to the mines.

He travelled to Nanaimo on Vancouver Island, where a number of his cousins were working in the coalmines and easily got a job although he had no experience as a miner. He threw himself into the work. It was hard but he came into contact with very exciting and interesting men. Often these fellow workers had lots of experience, were widely read and discussed a wide variety of matters. In turn they got him interested in politics. The area had become a hot-bed of socialist discussion and activity. He couldn't get over how well-read so many of his fellow workers were.

The local coalfield was dominated by owners who resisted trade unionism and ran a harsh regime in their mines. As industrial activity became more difficult, many of the miners became radicalised in their political beliefs. In 1901, in an attempt to satisfy these demands the British Columbia Socialist Party had been formed but even this was not sufficiently revolutionary for some of the miners who in turn formed their own Revolutionary Socialist Party.

William became caught up with all this political activity and in particular fell under the influence of Herbert Skinner who was thirty or so years his elder.

> He wasn't a working man in the sense that I had been. He was an English aristocrat. I don't know why he went out there in fact but he did and settled down. He was a socialist at heart and he wanted to do something for the cause. He had a rowing boat and on a Sunday he used to take me and another fellow over onto a smaller island and we used to study politics, philosophy and religion and all those sorts of subjects. That was a great influence on me and I have some books upstairs yet. Now he and I founded at that time, what turned out to be, the Social Democratic Party of Canada. He was the president and I was the secretary. I can remember drawing up the letter head and on that was a red flag, symbol of the one mass of humanity and also a quotation from Upton Sinclair, 'If a man today is not a revolutionary socialist he is either ignorant of civilisation or not honest'.

The Social Democratic Party was founded in 1911 and was composed largely of Finns, Swedes and British and was based along the lines of the

British and Scandinavian Labour Parties. As such it was very much a reformist and not primarily a revolutionary party. As such there was a determination for electoral success by socialist candidates. Parker Williams had been successful for Ladysmith and Jack Place for Nanaimo in the elections to the Legislature of British Columbia. Another successful candidate was Jimmy Haythornthwaite who was a larger than life character. He had made his fortune in the gold-rush but was still a socialist although he was eventually expelled from the socialist party allegedly for speculating in coal properties. However the three socialists held the balance of power between the Conservatives and Liberals and managed to get legislation of an eight hour day for miners.

There were a number of mines in the vicinity with a great demand for people to work in them. Labour was in short supply and in fact a number of Asians had been shipped in to help in the work. Labour relations were atrocious and the Asians were seen to exacerbate the problem as they were more compliant than the workers from Europe.

The principal mine-owner in the district was Robert Dunsmuir who was a 'poor lad made good'. But he had prospered by being an uncompromising employer and ran a tough regime. In particular he abhorred trade unions and would not tolerate them in his mines. The mines were known to be extremely dangerous and over the years there had been scores of accidents and explosions causing hundreds of miners to lose their lives or be seriously injured. Most of these accidents were caused by managerial shortcomings in the way explosives were handled. In 1887 in one major explosion, one hundred and fifty workers were killed. There was no social support in the event of an accident and the miners and their families were very much afraid of such happenings. All this added to the industrial unrest and accompanying left-wing political activity.

During the first year when William worked in the mine and was at the same time caught up in socialist politics, there developed a simmering discontent amongst the workforce. There were a number of factors involved; the fear of safety, falling wages partly as a result of the Asian workers accepting lower wages and the development of blacklisting for those seen as trouble-makers by the owners. In 1912, the Dunsmuirs sold their mines to a consortium led by Donald Mann, a leading figure in the building of the Canadian Pacific Railways. He made it clear however that he would continue with the same reactionary industrial relation policies as the previous owners. Many of the campaigners felt this was the very time to test the mettle of the new owners.

There was another factor in that the United Mineworkers of America (UMWA), which was a powerful syndicalist trade union over the border in the USA, had ambitions to extend their organisation throughout North America. It had been quietly recruiting members in British Columbia and now felt this was an appropriate moment to act in the Vancouver area. The event which sparked a strike was the blacklisting of a worker and a lockout of the miners in the nearby township, appropriately named, Cumberland. So in September 1912, the 'Great Strike', as it is remembered, began.

William Watson, the young immigrant from Cumbria, who was by now very politically aware, was immediately caught up in the dispute. Graphically he explains his initial involvement,

> There was no union at all and the United Mineworkers of America was spreading its wings you know and enlarging its territory, British Columbia wasn't organised, no union at all, so they sent up propagandists and Bob Harlin was one of them and he called a meeting of the miners to demand recognition of the union. It was decided that if they wouldn't agree then we would go on strike and we did. We went on strike and decided to appoint local officials. I remember the first big meeting and there were thousands there. There were four mines and maybe two or three hundred working in each. There was a big mass meeting and it came to the appointment of the secretary and somehow or other, I was appointed. There were Germans, Austrians, Norwegians, Finns and almost every nationality in Western Europe and to think that I should be chosen from all those. I thought it was a great honour.

William had no previous trade union organisational involvement. It seems likely that there were probably two principal reasons why he was chosen. Doubtless, as the UMWA was responsible for overall organisation and for the strike pay, their organisers would have some influence on the appointments locally. That a key union officer, Bob Harlin, was from the village of Pica in West Cumberland, only a couple of miles from Arlecdon, meant that he looked favourably on William. There had been a previous abortive attempt to unionise the mine a short time previously and the then secretary, Arthur Jordan, had ended up in prison. Jordan was from yet another village in Cumberland, Moresby near Whitehaven. In addition, there were a large number of Cumbrians at the Nanaimo mine including William's cousins. A further reason why Harlin may have been more comfortable with him was simply politics. The area around Nanaimo was well known for left-wing political activity with various sects and groups of a revolutionary socialist nature. Whilst William would have been known to be politically active, it was increasingly with the new Social Democratic Party of Canada. This was a more reformist organisation than its revolutionary rivals. The UMWA might have been more comfortable with his approach, especially given the electoral success which was being achieved.

But whatever the reasons, the new secretary threw himself into the struggle and learned quickly. The strike began reasonably peacefully but as time went on, it turned bitter. The company brought in blacklegs and violence broke out between these and the strikers. The militia and the local constabulary favoured the strike breakers and one striker was stabbed. As the bitterness grew so did the violence. Eventually a riot occurred and sections of the town were burned. Arrests were made and two strikers were sent to prison where one of them died. This in turn increased the wider support for the strikers but to no avail for by this time it was clear that the owners were not going to concede an inch and increasingly some of the miners drifted back to work. Others hung on, including the secretary, and after two and a half years the dispute ended in failure. The unionisation of the mines was to wait until the 1930s. William decided not to go back to the mine. 'Rather than go back, rather than ask for work, I came back here. I came back home'. The lessons of that long bitter strike were to remain with him for the rest of his life.

In 1915, William returned to an England that was in the midst of World War I where the demand for steel for munitions was insatiable. Thus there were plenty of employment opportunities for a worker in a limestone quarry as the product was an essential element in the manufacture of steel. He was also in a reserved occupation and thus not required for military service. Perhaps this was just as well for he was known to have doubts about the war and later was to campaign actively for the ending of hostilities by negotiation not fighting. He was allowed to return to his old job in Rowrah Hall Quarry.

To his delight, he discovered that his old school friend, Jack Adams, had recently returned after five years working in the coalmine at Runanga in New Zealand. More importantly he too had been converted to socialism. It is fascinating that the two men had left the same village five years previously and travelled to different countries in search of a better life only to have similar experiences and to return committed socialists. Whilst William had come across many remarkable individuals in the mines of Western Canada, Jack in New Zealand had been similarly influenced by Bob Semple and Paddy Webb on the industrial front whilst politically he had been impressed by Harry Holland who published the *Maoriland Worker*. He had become active in the emerging New Zealand Labour Party. For the next forty-five years, the lives of the two men were intertwined and when Jack died in 1960, William was appointed one of his executors.

Later Jack was to have an eminent career in Labour politics. In turn he was to be a district councillor, a county councillor and eventually a member of the House of Lords as Baron Adams of Ennerdale. He became a full-time official of his union, the Colliery Windingmen's Association, which he eventually gave up in 1935 to become the secretary and manager of the West Cumberland Industrial Development Company Ltd. Throughout his years of fighting for the rights of working people, he became widely respected and admired throughout the district. Indeed the local newspaper termed him 'King of Cumbria'.

The political scene locally had changed much since they had emigrated. In the next constituency to where they both lived, Whitehaven, there was a Labour MP. Tom Richardson, a miner from the North East of England had been returned in the election of December 1910 in a straight fight with the Conservatives. An accommodation had been reached with the Liberal Party in Cumberland that they would not contest Whitehaven if Labour reciprocated in the neighbouring seat of Cockermouth. The result was successful for the respective parties. Richardson proved to be very acceptable to the two young socialists for he had been a long-time member of the Independent Labour Party (ILP) which was on the left of the Labour Party. However, as both the local weekly newspapers, the *Whitehaven News* and the *Workington Star* were increasingly publishing photographs of young men killed in the war, Richardson was beginning to have a difficult time with many of his constituents in view of his opposition to the War.

In the local elections there had been an increase in Labour representation during the years when the two men were abroad. West Cumberland had been well to the fore in electing representatives of working people to local councils. As early as 1890, the Cumberland Labour Federation had been formed to provide financial assistance to cover loss of wages of elected Labour candidates. But the definition of what constituted 'Labour' was very loose and not all in this grouping could be described as socialist. Nevertheless, it did help facilitate the election of working men.

Until the revision of the Labour Party rules which came into force in 1918, there were no individual members. Prior to then, membership of the Party was through an affiliated body, usually a trade union or the ILP. There had been a longstanding branch of the ILP in Workington under the able leadership of two stalwarts Councillors Alfred Baines and Pat Walls. This was the constituency in which Jack and William lived and they were in contact with the branch there. There had been ILP activity in the years around the turn of the twentieth century and by the time William had left for Canada there were ten branches in West Cumberland. But at that stage of his life, he had no interest in politics. However, the ILP both locally and nationally went through a difficult period leading up to the outbreak of the war but by 1915 interest was beginning to revive.

This was the environment in which William began to play an active part in politics in Britain. He found a soul-mate in Jack Adams and also came in touch with another young man who had not travelled overseas but was also by then a convinced socialist, Bob Rigg, who lived a few miles north in the village of Broughton.

In William's words,

> While Jack had been active there (New Zealand) and I had in Vancouver, Bob Rigg also had been active here and he shouldn't be left out of the issue. He was a coal miner and he was a social-

ist. He was a very hard worker for the movement and he was a man who put far more into it than he ever got out of it. Now you couldn't say that of Jack Adams because Jack got a lot from it. Bob didn't. I often thought he should have had more.

The three young men acted as a team and they all cycled between the industrial villages spreading the message. They regarded socialism as their religion and threw themselves into propaganda work. The ILP was almost their lives and William said, 'I felt sure it was going to revolutionise the whole world. It's an exaggeration of course now I look back on it. That's the way I felt just then, that I had got hold of some eternal truth'.

The ILP centrally had decided that West Cumberland was fertile ground for expansion and encouraged the young activists. The regional organiser was sent across from Newcastle for a two-week spell to help promote the Party in the summer of 1916 and this quickly bore fruit. The *Labour Leader* had reported in January 1916 that a branch at Egremont was functioning (*Labour Leader*, 20 January 1916) and following the summer campaigning, a new branch was established in Broughton with Bob Rigg as secretary (*Labour Leader*, 14 September 1916). Two months later it was reported that there were two further branches at Cleator Moor and Whitehaven (*Labour Leader*, 16 November 1916). Progress was being made and the work of the three activists paying dividends.

Whilst the political work was progressing, William was also equally active on the industrial front. Following his experiences during the miners' strike in Canada he had learned a great deal and found the organisation in the quarries at home somewhat lacking. He had lost no time in getting involved. The local union was the Cumberland Limestone Quarrymen's Association and there was a full-time local official, Willie Cowen, whom William found not to be matching up to his ambitious ideals.

He was a Primitive Methodist local preacher and I should say that would be his chief qualification for the job. But he wasn't very progressive industrially…He was Labour but the ILP would have been too radical, too progressive for him. … We didn't like their administration, we didn't like the officers, they were all stick-in-the-mud, I thought they just stood in the way of progress.

He was probably being unfair on Cowen who was to become Treasurer of the Whitehaven Divisional Labour Party when it was formed in April 1918 and later became a Labour councillor. Furthermore he attended the inaugural national meeting of the reformed Labour Party in January 1918 as the delegate from the Quarrymen's Association. In truth William was impatient in regard to the older man but it does serve to illustrate the tension between the idealistic and radical ILP and the more measured approach of the Labour Party and the trade unions. This tension was to raise its head repeatedly in the years ahead and especially in relation to attitudes towards the First World War.

Before long however, William's enthusiasm had won the support of his workmates and he was elected branch secretary and began attending wider union meetings becoming well-known throughout the union. In 1918, at the age of 30, he was elected President of the Cumberland Limestone Quarrymen's Association. As one of the local activists commented, it was the first honour that any of them had achieved. However his career in the union was to be short-lived for his activities were curtailed abruptly after five years.

Meanwhile things were happening on the electoral front. In early 1916, a vacancy occurred on the Arlecdon and Frizington Urban District Council following the death of one of the councillors. During the war years there was an electoral truce which meant that wherever possible elections should be avoided and any vacancies filled by co-option. Jack Adams was quickly off the mark and wrote putting forward his own name as a possible councillor. Whilst this seemed by many as preposterous, there were no other candidates. On the day when the issue was due to be discussed, there had been a bitter dispute amongst the councillors on a completely separate matter and when the vacancy came up, Jack was the beneficiary of the resulting fallout, and was elected by three votes to two with two abstentions! The young local socialists were delighted. They had one of their number sitting as a councillor. Now everything became a little more real. The following year, there was another death and Jack managed to get one of his colleagues onto the council, so there were now two Labour councillors.

Throughout the remaining years of the war, the young friends continued with their frenzied activities. Jack may already have married his sweetheart Annie and William was still courting his Sarah who lived a dozen miles away, but this did not distract them from their political work. They planned and dreamed how they were going to bring socialism to their part of West Cumberland. Cycling was the main means of travelling around the district. Bob Rigg, who lived in Broughton would cycle the five or so miles to Arlecdon or Rowrah, perhaps chair a meeting, have a follow-up discussion with his comrades and then cycle back home to be ready for the first shift at Buckhill Colliery early the following morning.

But it wasn't only short distances they travelled by bicycle. William Watson recalls cycling on several occasions to Newcastle; a distance of about one hundred miles. They would set off from Arlecdon after work on a Friday evening and travel overnight across the Pennines, attend an ILP meeting on Saturday and then make the return journey that same evening, arriving back in West Cumberland in the early hours of the Sunday. They did travel by train however to the ILP Conference at Leeds in April 1917 but the finances were so short that Jack Adams, Bob Rigg and William shared the same bed in a boarding house. Such was the dedication of the young men. It wasn't surprising that the regional organiser of the Labour Party in Newcastle saw great potential in the villages of West Cumberland.

To add even extra interest to the political debate, women's suffrage was becoming a bigger issue. The parliamentary secretary of the National Union of Women's Suffrage Societies, Catherine Marshall, lived in nearby Keswick where there was an active branch. The miners of Cumberland were regarded as amongst the most supportive of the miners' unions to the women's cause. In spring 1916, the suffrage societies launched a propaganda campaign in the local mining district and coincidentally at this time Marshall left the Liberals and joined the ILP in May 1916 (*Labour Leader*, 18 May 1916). She was to play quite a part in the ILP in the area being a delegate from the Broughton and Egremont branches to the 1921 and 1922 Annual Conferences (ILP, *Annual Conference Reports*, 1921, 1922).

This activity coincided with a growth of pro-war sentiment. Although miners and others involved in essential war-work were excused military service, many of the younger miners fulfilled what they saw as their patriotic duty, and joined up. So many young men in fact enlisted that there were insufficient left to mine the iron-ore and coal. The local trade union leaders were called to meet the minister responsible, Winston Churchill, to discuss what could be done to persuade some of the young men in uniform to return to the mines. Eventually some soldiers were persuaded to return in the national interest.

However, as the casualties grew so did the feeling against those who opposed the war, among them the Whitehaven MP, Tom Richardson. The shortage of recruits forced the government to introduce legislation in 1916 for conscription which divided the Labour movement as much as the country. At the beginning of January 1916, the local Egremont branch of the ILP reported that they were to have a special meeting which would be ... 'the last occasion on which it is possible to meet before certain of our members go up for training under Lord Derby's Scheme'. This was followed by a paper by Willie Cowen on 'When the Boys Return'. There is little doubt that William and his friends were at that meeting (*Labour Leader*, 20 January 1916).

Early in March 1916, Tom Richardson was being attacked in the local press for being anti-war and for voting against the Military Services Act which introduced conscription and he was charged that he 'knows no nationality' (*Whitehaven News*, 12 March 1916). The patriotic feeling was increasing, bordering on hysteria, and there was even a report that, 'a coloured man was charged with entering the protected part of Cumberland' (*Whitehaven News*, 16 June 1916). As the months went by, he had several difficult meetings in various parts of the country and then in July 1917 he had a particularly rough meeting in Whitehaven itself with the result that he was attacked and the house in which he had sought refuge was stoned with many windows being broken. The police arrested the trouble makers who were later charged and found guilty (*Whitehaven News*, 8 August and 6 September 1917). But this gives some indication of the hostility the opponents of the war faced. At about this time an effort was made by one of the non-conscription bodies to have a series of meetings against the war, in the Workington area, but most of these either ended in disputes or had to be abandoned.

There is a report that at a meeting of Arlecdon and Frizington Council in July 1916, a pro-war resolution was passed unanimously with Jack Adams remaining silent (Carruthers, p.38).

The young activists were having a difficult time with this issue. Gradually, as a number of clergymen, such as Rev. Dunnico and Rev. Moll, visited the area and addressed ILP meetings, a clearer approach based on peace negotiations began to take shape. Perhaps the stance could be best illustrated by a Rowrah ILP meeting in June 1917 with William in the chair, when the following resolution was passed unanimously,

> In the opinion of this meeting the time has now arrived when the Allied Powers should re-state their war aims so as to bring them into agreement with those of the Russian and American Governments with the object of securing a negotiated peace at the earliest possible moment.

Reverend Dunnico went on to stress that he was 'not in favour of a patched-up peace. Before peace could be proclaimed there should be complete indemnification of Belgium by the Germans and the evacuation of French Territory' (*Whitehaven News*, 21 June 1917). Not exactly revolutionary but it proved divisive amongst the British people.

They made one last public foray in 1917 on this issue which was enthusiastically reported in the *Whitehaven News*,

> On August Bank Holiday Monday great excitement was caused on the shore at St Bees by the meeting held by the members of the Cumberland ILP. Having made a stand, and with the Red Flag flying the meeting commenced by the singing of one of their songs, followed by different speakers trying to get a hearing. Until it was seen they intended the demonstration in support of 'Peace by Negotiation, without Annexation', the speakers were attentively listened to, if not with approval with indifference. Bob

Rigg was in the chair and William was one of the speakers but it was Jack Adams for one of the few times in his life who was forced to stand down as he was well into moving the resolution on economic profiteering and peace proposals. The miners' leader from Whitehaven, J Hanlon, attempted to rescue the meeting but a Union Jack was produced from amongst the crowd and 'Rule Britannia' was sung. It began to get nasty and the speakers were forced to abandon the meeting under a hail of sods.

The local newspaper again captures the mood accurately,

The Red Flag was not in much evidence after this, and the few supporters of the ILP were obliged to disperse for safety, out of the way of the angry crowd. Apart from the few supporters of the ILP, there was very little sympathy shown for the views expressed, women especially being very strongly opposed to the views of the speakers (*Whitehaven News*, 9 August 1917).

William Watson claimed that this was the only time in his life, when he or Jack Adams, were ever 'sodded-off' a platform. But they understood the dangers of alienating people too greatly when they were trying to build a local political party and appealing for their votes. The experience was a lesson well-learned and their energies were redirected to this goal.

But William had also another life-changing event looming. On 27 September 1917, he was to marry his long-standing sweetheart, Sarah Johnston, at Gilcrux, a village a few miles to the north. Sarah's father was a colliery engineman but there were fifty guests at the wedding including of course Jack Adams, Bob Rigg and their wives. They were to remain happily married for almost seventy years and Sarah shared his politics and worked very hard in helping to build up support for Labour in West Cumberland. In those days when they had visiting speakers, in order to reduce the expenses, they were put up in the houses of supporters. The Watsons had a fairly large house by local standards and Sarah did more than her fair share of entertaining visiting speakers. In fact one of her favourite visitors was a guest at the wedding who gave them a copy of the 'Rubaiyat of Omar Khayyam' which they kept until their deaths. The individual in question was Joe Maxwell who was an MA from Leicester

University, and originally from Clydeside. In William's own words, 'He was a conscientious objector and was called-up. But he wouldn't go and the police were harassing him so he left home and had been all over the country; a fugitive from justice. And he stayed with us for weeks. Joe Maxwell and his wife Kathleen. She was Irish'.

On his return from Canada, William lived with his parents who had moved across the main road to the hamlet of Rowrah Hall. When he got married William had to bring his bride to live with his parents until they could get a house of their own. Unfortunately, to his disappointment the married couple's new address was literally just outside the Arlecdon and Frizington Urban District boundaries which of course meant that he was ineligible to stand for that council alongside his friend Jack. However his younger brother Walter, still lived within the district and stood for the council. Eventually after a two year wait the couple moved to their own home which of course was back in the urban district.

But with the political truce in place during the war there was no opportunity to test Labour's electoral strength. So the young activists concentrated on building up the ILP and Labour Party. Bob Rigg who had not spent time abroad was first to form a new branch of the ILP, at Broughton in September 1916 and it was no surprise that he was elected the secretary (*Labour Leader*, 14 September 1916).

The Cumberland Federation of the ILP met in Workington in October and decided to concentrate on existing weak branches. Cleator Moor, Egremont, Kendal and Whitehaven were identified. But the Broughton Branch was very active and increasingly successful and by Christmas 1916 counted on forty-one members. Meanwhile in addition to attending the Broughton Branch, Jack and William were beavering away at trying to establish a branch at Rowrah and in April 1917 they were successful with William becoming secretary (*Labour Leader*, 3 May 1917).

Their enthusiasm was not diminished and the branch went from strength to strength with growing membership and weekly meetings and by November 1917 they had attracted one hundred members (*Labour Leader*, 15 November 1917). Throughout the remaining years of the Great War, the Rowrah Branch continued with a host of activities in addition to the weekly political meetings. Social evenings, dances and teas became regular features more often than not with visiting speakers. The wives were now much involved and the new Mrs Sarah Watson was much in evidence. Whist Drives also became a popular event as the ILP really became the heart of the working-class community. This was recognised by the *Labour Leader* when it reported that,

> Sunday evening found [Bruce] Glasier and [Tom] Richardson at Rowrah. Here a vigorous branch, nearly 100 strong, has come into existence during the present year, in a small village away in the Cumberland hills. A crowded room listened with intense interest to the inspiring address on 'Internationalism' given by Glasier (*Labour Leader*, 15 November 1917).

During 1918, the Labour Party was undergoing a reorganisation, it created new constituency parties which included trade unions, affiliated socialist societies and branch parties composed of individual members for the first time ever. Whitehaven was first to be established locally on 6 April 1918 and Gavan Duffy, the general secretary of the Iron Ore Miners' Union from neighbouring Cleator Moor, was selected as the prospective Parliamentary Candidate for the following general election (*Whitehaven News*, 11 April 1918). Tom Richardson, the sitting MP had decided not to contest the seat again much to the disappointment of the young ILPers who had identified with his political stance.

Of Gavan Duffy, William said that he had beaten the then full-time official of the Iron Ore Miners' Union for the secretary's position and was 'very brainy',

> Gavan had a good knowledge of compensation law and he did a lot of good work for the miners. What he did for them industrially showed itself politically when Gavan was adopted as candidate. He was a good friend in some ways was Gavan but he had a nasty habit of antagonising his friends sometimes. He did that with nearly everybody. He did it with Jack Adams and he did it with me.

William recalls moving the resolution to establish the Workington Divisional Labour Party a little later in September 1918 when Tom Cape was chosen as the parliamentary candidate (*Workington Star*, 20

September 1918). Cape was secretary of the Cumberland Miners' Association and well known locally but his politics were quite different to Richardson's. In particular he had distanced himself from Richardson's position on the war and this was to be instrumental during the ensuing election. During the successful campaign, William spoke on a number of platforms in support of Tom Cape. When the general election came in December 1918, the ILP in the villages surrounding Workington worked incessantly and probably made the difference between success and failure as Cape won for Labour.

William said of the campaign meetings and the MP,

> Well they were good. They were enthusiastic and you sort of read a conviction and if I sow something in this soil there's a chance that it might grow and it did. It ended up with Tom being elected and it continued until the end of his career. He was never a spectacular MP you know, but he was sound and a good hard worker.

Tom Cape proved to be very popular with his constituents, being returned for seven successive elections including an unopposed return in 1935 until he retired in 1945.

Following this electoral success there was little time before they had the county council elections to fight in March 1919. Their emphasis was on Jack Adam's attempt to unseat the established county councillor and local squire, Thomas Dixon of Rheda Hall. He did so, gaining the seat relatively easily by 500 votes (*Whitehaven News*, 13 March 1919). Labour was beginning to make enemies but Jack was to prove immovable and was to remain on Cumberland County Council until his death forty-one years later.

But the young men and women had plans for something even more audacious. With the wartime truce having finished, all the local council seats became vacant and the local Labour Party decided to contest every one of them. The election organisation was well-proven and the candidates were well known to the electors but it was a great surprise to everyone except the local ILP when Labour won every single seat. Arlecdon and Frizington Urban District Council had become the first council in

England where every councillor was Labour. To William's frustration and disappointment he was still ineligible to stand because of his address being just outside the council boundary but his younger brother, Walter was elected (*Whitehaven News*, 10 April 1919).

The ensuing three years saw the councillors determined to prove that Labour Councils were different. Jack Adams became the chair and great changes happened. The local council workers were given a wage increase and May Day was declared a public holiday. The councillors were deeply worried about the health of the local children, fell out with the Medical Officer of Health, sacked him and doubled the pay of his replacement. They were concerned over the quality of meat supplied to the council and started building the first council houses in Cumberland. It was an eventful period during which Jack Adams lost his job and although staying on the council he eventually had to resign as the chair (*Whitehaven News*, 28 April 1920).

One thing was certain, they had proved that a Labour council was different. Three years later the local establishment had reorganised itself electorally and that, coupled with a number of sitting Labour members deciding not to fight again, meant that Labour was reduced to four councillors. One of these was William Watson who had by this time moved back into the district. But they immediately ran into a complicated situation.

At the inaugural meeting of the new council, the Labour Group proposed one of the Independents as chair, attracting five votes to the opposition's four. The chairman, the former local headmaster, ruled that their motion was lost as he was not accepting the votes of three of the Labour councillors, as he considered them ineligible to be councillors as they had received 'poor law relief' sometime during the previous twelve months. The chair declared that electors had alerted him to the fact that certain members had received this poor relief and that some gentlemen had called upon him and pointed out that if anyone voted who was disqualified they 'intended to take proceedings against them'. The local establishment seemed to have done their homework and were determined to exclude the elected Labour councillors by fair means or foul. The Clerk read out the section of the Local Government Act which seemed to disqualify the councillors. In response Cllr Watson, who was not one of those who had received poor relief, accused the chair of intimidation and the Labour councillors declared they had been through the due electoral process, fairly elected and indeed declared elected by the returning officer. An impasse was reached and the meeting broke up in disorder.

The *Whitehaven News* had a field day. Under the headline 'A Sensational Affair', it ran the following story,

> No political stage drama of recent times has been so pregnant of sensational moves and counter-moves as the annual meeting of the Arlecdon and Frizington Council held on Friday night. Animation was introduced to the proceedings following nomination for the office of chairman of Mr Laidlaw (who at the recent election ran as an Independent candidate) by the four Labour members… (*Whitehaven News*, 27 April 1922).

The story was to run and run as the issue appeared to have raised complicated and nonsensical legal rulings. Labour threats to resign and pleas for them not to, came and went. The Independent councillors were not keen to have by-elections fearing that the Labour candidates might attract even more sympathy votes following the disqualifications. The matter went on for several months without resolution until eventually the matter was allowed to fizzle out and the Labour councillors were eventually accepted as having been properly elected. Apparently there was a great deal of local feeling for them but it does illustrate the determination of the local establishment to stop Labour at all costs. However on this occasion they may well have overstepped the mark with the electors siding with the Labour councillors (*Whitehaven News*, 4, 11, 18 May 1922).

The issue rumbled on under the surface, and in 1925 William Watson was elected vice-chairman and finally in April 1928, none of the Independents were prepared to stand for the chair and as a result, he was elected chairman unanimously (*Whitehaven News*, 25 April 1928).This was a popular choice for he was a much respected figure and he held the post for eight years. He was now a prominent local figure for he had been made the manager of the five quarries in the vicinity. In December 1920, the owners had realised his knowledge, intelligence and ability and offered him the post. Although initially he and Sarah were undecided for they were so much committed to working for the socialist cause, eventually he decided to accept the offer. As he later explained,

> When the job was offered to me as quarry manager, I didn't know
> whether to take it or not. They might think I was doing wrong,
> going over to the boss's side if I take it. And I put it to the men
> and I told them what had happened. I told them that this offer
> had been made to me and asked them whether I should accept it
> or not. They unanimously thought it would be in my best inter-
> ests to accept it and also the interests of the people I was repre-
> senting. So I did accept it and because of that I was getting, not
> a good salary, but a decent one. I was better off than those
> around me financially.

He had ascertained that he would still be allowed to pursue his politics
and he remained as active as ever. If he had had to choose he would have
chosen to remain in the Labour movement. However, he had to give up
his union activities including the presidency. But in the longer run he had
found being the manager helpful and useful, 'I was the only one who had
experience of sitting on both sides of the table; first as representative of
the men and then later on the employer's side'.

Over fifty years later, when asked whether he thought he had been right
to accept the job in hindsight he was very positive,

> They said that I should have this job. Well it later turned out they
> were right. I did well to accept it or otherwise there would have
> been more hunger than there was. They were pleased to accept
> bread. There was a lot of poverty in the thirties, oh lots of pover-
> ty. A lot of people that we knew and they would come to our
> house. Oh dear. I should say you've no idea just how bad things
> were. People used to come round for pennies to buy bread. Dry
> bread. A loaf of dry bread. The children were almost bare-foot-
> ed.

Amidst all this poverty, the local stalwarts continued to bring in propagandists, most of who stayed with the Watsons in their terrace house
which although having four large bedrooms, was without a bathroom. A

whole string of party visitors stayed with them and many became good friends. The list is like a litany of early Labour stars including; Rev. H Dunnico, Bruce and Katherine Glasier, Sheila MacDonald, Jimmy Maxton, Joe Maxwell, Reverend W E Moll, Walton Newbold, Minnie Pallister, Mannie Shinwell, Dick Spears, Jessie Stephens, Harry Stobbart, Dick Wallhead and his daughter, James Walsh and Wilfred Wellock and his wife, and many others. Some they liked better than others. Bruce Glasier was one favourite. William remembered,

> Now he came several times and I remember the last time he came and I knew it was his last, poor old fellow. I remember he caught hold of the beam to stand up, he was so frail. You could see that he was going downhill and this would be his last visit. I remember Bruce very well…Oh we liked Bruce Glasier. Oh yes we did indeed. He was good, he was sound. I liked his sincerity. He had a good heart and he had a good brain. I liked Bruce very well and we also liked his wife, Katharine…We used to call her Kath of the Bruce. She was very nice. She had her breakfast in bed.

On the other hand there was one person of whom they did not approve and that was Walton Newbold, eventually the first elected Communist MP (Motherwell) in 1922.

> He stayed with us and Mrs Watson was too good to him. She made things so very comfortable and fed him so well that one night he should have gone to Parton to conduct a meeting and he feigned illness didn't he? He asked us to go and send a telegram to Parton but Mrs Watson wouldn't. She said you're not ill and you're going to the meeting. He went on the bus.

In spite of the intense poverty throughout the district, William recalled the friendships they formed in those days with immense affection,

> I don't think there were many tears. There was a lot of joy. Oh yes, we met some splendid people. Where would you get a better man than Wilfred Wellock or James Walsh. Without our common

love for the movement, we wouldn't have known Jimmy Walsh or Wilfred Wellock. It was the road into their real characters. We liked them very much. We would have our meeting in Arlecdon and then we would go down the mile and a half to Frizington. We walked down for a big meeting at the Palace Picture House. Very good. Sheila MacDonald went down there. We didn't have money to print bills and I would write them out by hand. We put them on the notice board, put one in your window, put one in my window and that sort of thing. And we had the meetings on street corners and round railway bridges, that was our favourite place.

One of the most popular propagandists of this period was the former *Clarion* activist, Casey who used a rather different approach to get across the socialist message as William recalls,

Casey's first qualification of course was his ability to play the fiddle and he thought that was the biggest contribution that he could make to socialism. He was undoubtedly a socialist. He was on the road travelling up and down. I don't know if he had any home of his own. His proper name was Walter Hampson. Somehow or other he came across Dolly who was young enough to be his daughter. They travelled about together all over the country. I don't know what her second name was, I don't think they were related at all. She played the piano and Casey the violin and they were very good players. They used to intersperse their playing with just a few remarks from themselves along socialist lines and then they would play something else. He was very popular. I remember presiding for him.

The events of the Labour Government's downfall in 1931 left William fuming about Ramsay MacDonald's actions. Sarah was however more understanding. She had been one of his fans. She said, years later, 'He had real problems. He was a grand chap you know. He did his best'. She was more sympathetic but when the general election came they both voted for their constituency MP, Tom Cape. He was one of only fifty-two Labour MPs to be elected at that election. Workington had remained true to Labour so perhaps this was the result of the hard propaganda work that had taken place in the industrial villages over the years.

During the 1930s, like many other activists, the Watsons drifted away from the ILP and switched all their efforts to help the Labour Party rebuild itself after the debacle of 1931. They remained active and were present in 1945 to help select Fred Peart as the new Labour Candidate for Workington. Throughout the 1950s and 1960s they continued to play their part in the party. They also kept in close touch with Jack Adams and his wife long after he was elevated to the House of Lords. They served together as governors of the Whitehaven Secondary School and in the 1950s, the pair was still fighting battles side by side as they had forty years previously.

Seventy years on from his conversion to socialism, William Watson was invited to reflect on his beliefs and the passage of time and he did so initially by explaining,

> You see so much that's wrong, so much that needs mending, you think the only way to do it is not by a little, but truly to grasp the sorry state of things and smash it. I should say every socialist at times would feel like that. As it is so well expressed in the Rubayait of Omar Khayyam,

> Ah love could you and I with him conspire
> To grasp this sorry Scheme of Things entire,
> Would not we shatter it to bits and then
> Re-mould it nearer to our Heart's Desire.

> Joe Maxwell gave us that book when we got married.

Then in a spirit of hope, he outlined his dreams for the future by quoting two verses from his favourite Hymn 52 from the *Socialist Sunday School Tune Book*;

> These things shall be! A loftier race
> Than e'er the world hath known shall rise
> With flame of freedom in their souls,
> And light of science in their eyes.

These things - they are no dreams - shall be
For happier men when we are gone:
Those golden days for them shall dawn,
Transcending aught we gaze upon.

When he was in his nineties William Watson was asked if it had all been worth it and he replied succinctly,

Yes, yes it's been worth it David. I haven't realised everything I set out to do but it's been worth it. Mrs Watson sometimes says that if we had to go through it again, she couldn't entertain so many propagandists as she did in those days. She sometimes says that but I do really think it's been worth it. Oh yes indeed.

They both died within months of each other, as they approached their hundredth birthdays and after seventy years of marriage. Sarah who had been born on 26 January 1888 died on 6 January 1987 whilst William died just a month before his hundredth birthday on 26 July 1987.

Quotations of William Watson from interviews with David Clark on 8 March and 29 March 1979.

2

Frank William Parrott
1890-1986

It was the late afternoon of a beautiful early summer day in 1925. Frank William Parrott sat at the headmaster's desk in the Council School in Kirkby Stephen, a small town in Westmorland. He was just finishing the routine administrative chores of the school day and was feeling very satisfied with life. It had only been a short time since he had taken up the headship but he was beginning to feel he was making a difference. Suddenly, he was disturbed from his reverie by a loud knocking on the door. On opening it, he was confronted by two well-dressed ladies in large hats who inquired whether they might have a word with him.

Somewhat intrigued, he invited them in, found them seats and spent a few minutes in small talk. Before long his suspense was relieved when one of them surprised him by saying that they had come to collect his subscription. Somewhat perplexed, he inquired to what he was expected to subscribe. Instantly he was informed, 'The Westmorland Conservative Association'. Taken aback, he told his visitors that he did not subscribe to, or indeed support, the Conservative Party, only to be met with the immediate riposte, 'but you must Mr Parrott, all headmasters in Westmorland subscribe to the Conservative Association'.

The local establishment had chosen the wrong man in FW Parrott who was a convinced socialist and a paid-up member of both the Labour Party and the Independent Labour Party (ILP). As he later recounted this began a difficult period for him in the polite society of North Westmorland. 'It was bad enough not being a Conservative but it became even more difficult when they discovered I did not attend the Church of England. When it became known I was a vegetarian, I was branded as a crank and beyond the pale'.

A further manifestation of his deeply-held beliefs was evidenced by the new head's choice of newspaper. He ordered the Labour supporting *Daily Herald*, the only person to do so in Kirkby Stephen and the newsagent went to the chairman of his school managers advising him to keep an eye 'on that headmaster of yours. He's taking the *Daily Herald* '.

Throughout his life, Frank Parrott kept a diary and retained much data relating to his very full life. These are now preserved in thirty-six boxes in the Cumbrian Archives Service in Kendal and allows us to accurately follow his activities over the years (WDX 1846, CAC Kendal).

By the time of his death sixty-one years later however, he had undoubtedly become the most respected member of the local community. He had served on the parish council for thirty-seven years, the rural district council for twenty-one and the county council for fifteen. He had never suffered an election defeat. In addition he had become chair of the local magistrates. On his retirement, the clerk of the local council wrote to him, 'your record of service in all matters of life will not be equalled' (Box 26, letter 12 July 1973, CAC). All in all, it was a far cry from that summer day in 1925 for the avowed socialist headmaster.

Kirkby Stephen is a small market town with a population of a little under 2000, serving the Upper Eden Valley in what was formerly the County of Westmorland and is now Cumbria. It is the centre for a largely agricultural community and remains extremely busy on market days. It has always provided the retail base for the area with a reasonably wide range of shops and the usual service providers.

It is about thirty miles from the two larger towns of Kendal and Penrith. With development of motor vehicles as the twentieth century evolved, the road network became more important. The main road southwards through the town went to Lancashire whilst five miles to the north, it joined the main trans-Pennine road linking the north-east and north-west coasts of England.

For many years however, the railways were more important to the town. It was served by two railway stations; one belonging to the LMS, linked West Yorkshire with Carlisle and was situated a little over a mile from the town centre. It was opened in 1875 and is still in use today on the scenic Settle to Carlisle line which Frank Parrott was so instrumental in saving from closure in the 1980s. Certainly the more important politically belonged to the LNER which provided a service between the

North East and the West Coast. It was opened on 8 August 1861 but due to lack of traffic closed on 22 January 1962. This was a particularly important goods route with raw materials being transported between the heavy industrial areas of Durham, Newcastle and Tees-side and Cumbria. It also carried limestone from the local quarries to the iron and steel works on both the east and west coasts.

Railways however not only carried passengers and goods but they also conveyed political ideas and this was not to be unimportant to political life in Kirkby Stephen. Although the principal railway centre in the locality was twelve miles south at Tebay, many railwaymen from County Durham broke their journeys at Kirkby Stephen. That county was regarded as one of the strongholds of the Labour Party and indeed the Parliamentary Constituency of Barnard Castle was less than a dozen miles from the town and been won by Labour in a by-election as early as 1903. FW Parrott recalls that the local railwaymen exchanged political ideas in their mess room with their fellow workers from across the North East and were greatly influenced by them.

Although the area was dominated by farming there was a considerable amount of mining and quarrying for which the railways were vital. This was reflected in the religious culture of the town with a strong presence of non-conformity. Indeed the school board, which pre-dated the education committee, had always been finely balanced between supporters of the Church of England and the dissidents. Possibly remnants of this tradition could have been a factor in the appointment of FW Parrott.

Politically the area was strongly Conservative. From 1885 until 1918, Kirkby Stephen was part of the Westmorland Appleby Constituency, and the traditional local aristocrats, the Lowther family, had great influence. The Conservatives held the seat with the exception of the years between 1900 and 1910 when the Liberals were successful.

In 1918 with the extension of the franchise to include many more working men and for the first time some women, a new seat of Westmorland was created and the Conservatives were successful in each of the twenty-two General Elections of the twentieth century. Indeed for the first three of these they were not even challenged until 1924 when Reginald P Burnett, stood as the Labour Candidate attracting 7242 votes. The Labour Party in the county was ill-equipped to contest the seat with the Constituency Labour Party having only being formed on 28 June 1924 (Clark, 2012 p.82).

The candidate was frank enough to tell the local paper that six months prior to the election there was no constituency organisation. Then the party attempted to organise itself as a matter of urgency and a number of prominent speakers came to the area including Marion Phillips, the Party's national women's officer. Nevertheless the Conservative majority remained in excess of ten thousand. More national Labour Party figures periodically visited the constituency such as Philip Snowden in 1928 and the Labour activists in Westmorland unsuccessfully ran a candidate in the election of 1929. There was no contest in 1931 but FW Parrott was involved on Labour's behalf in the fourteen following contests but without success.

FW Parrott was not however from Kirkby Stephen nor indeed from the North of England. He was born on 31 December 1890 in the town of Wellingborough in Northamptonshire, far from where he was to spend most of his life. It was one of the centres of the boot and shoe industry. FW Parrott later explained, 'There was a strong radical feeling and it expressed itself through Liberalism in the main. Of course Father was a great admirer of Lloyd George and I remember Lloyd George coming to Wellingborough when I was a kid of twelve. But I got captured with the new movement and especially Keir Hardie'.

His father, also Frank, was a foreman in the warehouse of a large factory where they made nothing but boots with big export orders, especially from Ireland and America. His father was a highly respected and respectable working man. His job involved working much overtime and the young Frank often accompanied him where apparently he did a lot of reading. According to Frank, 'They were not highly paid. They never got more than 30 shillings (£1.50 per week). They had a very nice house, rented, overlooking the main valley'.

A flavour of the family upbringing young Frank received, can be gleaned from the obituary notices of his parents. His father was described as having been prominent locally in Methodism, Cooperation and Temperance. Furthermore he held the grandiose sounding title of District Chief Ruler of the Order of Rechabites, a temperance friendly society. His mother, Clara, was no less formidable having been for twenty years a board member of the Wellingborough Industrial Cooperative

Society and for thirty-three years president of the Wellingborough Women's Cooperative Guild. This service was recognised as so exceptional that she was later rewarded with the honour of life membership of the national organisation (Box 9, CAC).

The Parrotts were the archetypal aspiring working class family so praised in Victorian literature and the children were brought up very much within this ethos. They were sent to Sunday school, heard radical political debate in the household and generally were taught a liberal and tolerant view of society. Young Frank imbibed all these values with enthusiasm and became quite outspoken. This was evidenced many years later in 1983 when writing in *The Vegetarian*, 'On Sunday, July 26th 1903, I sat at the dinner table with my mother, father, sister and brother and surprised them by declaring, when mother was preparing our dishes that I did not want any meat either then or ever again'. Apparently this had not come as a real surprise to his mother as his Sunday school teacher had warned her a little earlier that 'I was developing queer notions and asking awkward questions'. Until his dying day, Frank never touched meat and his mother never tried to persuade him to do otherwise (*The Vegetarian*, July/August 1983).

For the times, they were a relatively small family of three children and in true Victorian ethos; education was regarded as being of prime importance. The young Frank received his elementary education at the Victoria School, Wellingborough, passing through all the 'standards' and becoming head boy. He enjoyed school as his reports indicate. As he was nearing the school-leaving age, the Education Act of 1902 was enacted and this required a large increase in the number of teachers and their training was to be revolutionised. The headmaster persuaded Frank's father that his son would make a good teacher and that he should be allowed to stay on at school. The progressively thinking family eventually agreed.

The young man stayed on at school until he was 15 and to help out with the family budget he took a part-time job as an errand boy at the local dye works. He was paid three shillings a week for working evenings and Saturdays. Apparently he was excused Saturday afternoons as he was generally regarded as a promising footballer. This was confirmed twenty-five years later in an article which appeared in the *Wellingborough News* which included the following extract, 'Mr Frank W Parrott, one of the greatest characters that local junior football has ever had - it would require a full article to pay tribute to all the service he rendered to football and the influence he had upon the game and players' (*Wellingborough News*, 15 October 1937). A fulsome and flattering tribute and many years later he was to play, inspire and captain the local Kirkby Stephen Harriers Football Club in the Westmorland League.

At fifteen, he was appointed a monitor at Westfield Boys School, Wellingborough. This was the first step in his progression towards the attainment of qualifications and he was paid the princely sum of £7.10 shillings a year. He was only in this position for two months for he then passed the Pupil Teacher Entrance Examinations and went to Wellingborough Pupil Teacher Centre. For two and a half years he attended the centre on a half-time basis and he was placed in local schools for the other half of his time to gain practical experience. At the end of the course he passed the Preliminary Examination which qualified him as an uncertified teacher. After temporary posts as an uncertified teacher he began a two year course at the City of Sheffield Teacher Training College in 1910 (Box 8, CAC).

On successfully completing his course he was selected as a teacher by London County Council. This was a prestigious appointment but meant that he wasn't appointed to a particular school; but as a qualified teacher was posted from school to school as the need arose. Today this would be regarded as similar to being a supply teacher but the key difference was that it was a permanent position. This lack of attachment to one school he found particularly unsettling and difficult. This proved to be an unhappy period which he described as 'one of the loneliest in my life'.

By then, he was very much under the twin influences of Methodism and socialism. He took advantage of being in the capital city to attend many political meetings and his London experiences only reinforced his socialist beliefs. In particular he enjoyed visiting the public gallery of the House of Commons to listen to his heroes; Ramsay MacDonald, Philip Snowden and his particular favourite, Keir Hardie whom he admired especially for 'his passion'. Whenever he could he went to Labour meetings and specifically recalls struggling through a 'pea-soup fog to get to the Albert Hall to hear George Bernard Shaw and Keir Hardie share a platform on the "War on Poverty".'

In 1913 he had the opportunity to transfer to a teaching job nearer his home at Bedford where he remained until November 1915. As a pupil teacher in his home town he had become active in the St John's Ambulance Brigade and on his return he revived this interest. This was to have a more significant effect on his life than he could have envisaged.

When war was declared in August 1914, the Army in Britain was initially inundated with recruits volunteering to do their patriotic duty. The young teacher did not share this patriotic fervour but it did not matter as he continued with his work as a teacher and redoubled his efforts with the St John's Ambulance Brigade in Wellingborough. By mid-1915 however, attitudes began to harden. It soon became clear that the War was going to last much longer than had been originally thought and there was a shortage of young men coming forward as volunteers. The political debate raged as to whether conscription should be introduced. Eventually in the autumn of 1915 a compromise position known as the 'Derby Scheme' was introduced which in essence required young men to pledge their enlistment at some future date. This was completely impractical and eventually the Military Service Act was passed on 27 January 1916 with conscription following very soon afterwards but public opinion remained divided.

By this time, Frank was an active member of the Independent Labour Party (ILP) sharing the Party's opposition to the war, arguing 'peace by negotiation'. In November 1915, at the height of this public discord, the Director of Education for Bedfordshire called him in and told him bluntly, 'You are not in the army so you have lost your job'.

Far from becoming dejected by his dismissal, the twenty-five year old Frank accepted it with equanimity. In fact it was probably a welcome happening. He was very much involved in the Methodist Church and the ILP and clearly had decided his position. He had become a conscientious objector. Daily the heat was being turned up on the non-combatants and the Director of Education's decision simply forced him into action.

Indeed, he may well have been expecting it. Although a conscientious objector, he was not an absolutist. Whilst he was not prepared to take up arms and kill people, he was prepared to play a part in relieving suffering. He had been increasingly active in the St John's Ambulance Brigade, becoming a qualified 'first aider and home nurse'. He was aware of the Friends' Ambulance Unit which sent young men out to the front line to assist with ambulance work. On his sacking he applied to join and was accepted in spite of the fact that he was not a Quaker but a Methodist.

He was sent to the Friends' Ambulance Unit training camp at Jordans near Beaconsfield. The camp is on the estate of one of the earliest purpose-built Friends' Meeting Houses which had belonged to the Penn family who founded Pennsylvania. The remnant of the camp remains in the idyllic Berkshire countryside and is now used by the Youth Hostels Association.

There, when the authorities learned of his experience as a physical training teacher, he was put in charge of keeping the other young men fit and healthy in addition to his routine training in medical and nursing matters. Then came a bombshell when the Government 'put an embargo on members of the St John's Ambulance who were not Quakers serving with the Friends' Ambulance Units in France. So I was sent up to the military hospital in York. I never did go before a tribunal for non-combatants'.

As this move occurred prior to the Military Service Act of 1916, Frank was not required to appear before a tribunal. His conscientious objection was based primarily on religious grounds reinforced by his socialist beliefs but the fact that he had volunteered to go and work as a nurse at a military hospital in York meant that he was excused the rigour of a tribunal appearance. He later said, 'I have wished I had (gone before a tribunal) but I think they took us en bloc as it were'.

He thoroughly enjoyed his time at Jordans and the experience began a slow shift in his religious convictions from Methodism to the Quakers. He wrote in his diary at the time, 'I left Jordans Camp, Beaconsfield, having spent five of the happiest weeks of my life' (Box 22, CAC). Frank kept a daily diary continuously from 1905 until his death but he left a note apologising that his diaries were incomplete for his period at Jordans as he had simply been too busy!

There had been a large military hospital at York for many years but Frank was sent to a newly opened annexe which was in the building which had formerly housed the staff dining facilities of the chocolate manufacturers, Rowntrees. He went there in January 1916 under a scheme jointly run under the auspices of the Red Cross, St John's Ambulance and the Friends' Ambulance Unit and remained until December 1918. He found the work on the wards very rewarding and whilst he was there he met and fell in love with a Scots nurse, Barbara

Sinclair Mactavish from Inverness. They were married at Acomb Friends' Meeting House in York on 11 August 1919.

Frank Parrott seated centre in the uniform of the Friends' Ambulance Unit at York Military Hospital,1917

Whilst working at the hospital in York, Frank Parrott continued with his wider interests. He adhered to his Christian beliefs whilst gradually moving further towards Quakerism. In politics he pursued his interest in socialism. He was an active member of the ILP, attending meetings and reading widely. He read very little of Karl Marx but one of the books which had first convinced him of the case for socialism was Robert Blatchford's *Merrie England*, which had been a publishing phenomenon in the 1890s. One penny-edition of the book sold over one million copies. As a teenager he found Blatchford most persuasive. As he later explained, 'I liked Blatchford, he was very convincing. I didn't like his wartime stance because he was an ex-soldier and when the war broke out I didn't like him. But I liked his *Clarion* newspaper and I used to go the library and read it'. Blatchford was reputed to have converted millions of people to socialism but, as the First World War approached, he became very patriotic and anti-German with no time whatsoever for conscientious objectors.

Another of his interests was education and this remained undiminished over his lifetime. He formed the belief, from which he never waivered, that only through education could the problems of the world be met. Indeed slightly later, when he was speaking during the 1923 General Election in support of the Labour candidate for York, J King, he said, 'The education policy of the Labour Party is far in advance of any other'. He continued, 'The Labour Party is essentially a young man's movement' (Box 11, CAC).

Through the contacts he had made in educational circles, he was successful in obtaining a teaching job in York after ceasing to work at the hospital on 31 December 1918. In January 1919, he took up a post as form- and house-master in Elmfield College which was a boarding school mainly for the sons of Primitive Methodist ministers. He enjoyed the work teaching geography, history, religious instruction and sport. Following his marriage he moved into a rented house near the school.

In the second half of 1924 the landlord informed Barbara and Frank that he needed the house and that they would have to leave. The result was that Frank started looking for another post. Initially he looked for positions nearer his home town in the Midlands but none materialised. Thus his attention switched to a vacancy in the council school at Kirkby Stephen which had the added advantage of having a house with the position, an attractive proposition for a married applicant. Rather surprisingly he was successful and the conservative, rural market town ended up with a radical and very committed socialist as its headmaster. After a somewhat turbulent period in the initial months, neither side was to regret the choice.

So, on the 1 March 1925, the rather sleepy council school found itself with a new headmaster who was in the van of educational thinking and practice. A man committed to the power of education, he passionately believed that 'there was one cure for public distress and that is public education'. He looked upon his job as being more than just running a school efficiently and effectively but in producing young people who had mastered the three 'r's and as a vehicle for turning out school leavers to service the needs of the local and wider society.

Frank was himself a great reader and keen to raise awareness in current affairs. Thus one of the first things he did on arriving at the school was to place an order with the local newsagent for the Quaker journal, *The Friend*, *The Times Educational Supplement* and the daily papers, the *Daily*

Herald, Daily Telegraph and *Manchester Guardian.* The new head was paying for these out of his own pocket. He explained, 'I always was a believer in my children reading, I used to have a reading stand and I told the children that reading articles would help them'. Many years later, Frank was to muse wryly on the fact that the newsagent, having greedily taken Frank's order, went to the school authorities and objected to what the new head was doing. Such was the narrow mindedness that Frank faced, but it brought home to him the amount of work he was going to have to do. As he confirmed, 'I had a feeling that I was coming to a politically backward atmosphere but it gave me joy to be involved in the pioneering work'.

Frank Parrott was a man of wide interests and threw himself into developing these in the village. In such a close knit community his influence soon began to have an effect. He had taken a decision to lead by example. He was a fine sportsman and joined the local cricket, football and hockey clubs and in time captained all three. This gave him a positive image in a community where education was not regarded very highly.

Whilst he was working at the hospital in York, Frank became friendly with the headmaster of the local elementary school who had been very concerned about the welfare of his senior pupils and ex-pupils. This was principally because many of their fathers were absent on active service whilst their mothers were often involved in munitions work. He had noted how effective old-boys' associations were in many public and grammar schools. As a result he had established such a body for his elementary school in York with considerable success, taking courses in first aid and physical exercise himself.

On taking over the school in Kirkby Stephen he found a similar problem with there being little provision for ex-pupils. After discussions with interested teachers he called a public meeting in September 1925 with the sitting county councillor, an ex-pupil, in the chair. He recorded that 'It was enthusiastically decided to form an Old Scholars' Association and the school became the centre of many social and cultural activities…Their first annual report mentioned the following activities:- first aid (nine qualified), home nursing (eleven qualified), gymnastics, handicrafts, wireless and electricity, sports clubs, community singing and socials'. Frank and his wife took the courses in first aid.

This initiative was a real brainwave and caught the imagination of the local people, many of whom gave the initiative their support. The real strength of the Association was that it provided such a broad range of interests thus appealing to a wide section of the community. The Association continued along similar lines with unpaid tutors until the local parish council established an evening class committee. That body ran courses with salaried tutors and some of the Association's classes then fell within their remit. During the Second World War activity faded and the Association gradually became a thriving dramatic society. But Frank Parrott had achieved a milestone through gaining the confidence and trust of many in the local community. Later this was to enable him to move further into even more ambitious projects.

Throughout the latter part of 1925 and the early months of the following year the new headmaster's stock continued to rise. In May 1926 however, progress was threatened. On the 3 May a General Strike was declared across the country by the trade union movement and a number of the workers in sleepy Kirkby Stephen were affected.

One specific group which was involved in the General Strike was the railwaymen who prided themselves in their sense of solidarity and also as being in the van of the labour movement. They were using the Temperance Hall, just around the corner from the local council school, as their strike headquarters. Four days after the beginning of the strike, they approached the headmaster for advice and assistance because they were '…fed-up of hearing each other tell dirty stories and wasting time. Can you give us a talk on anything you like?' The headmaster readily agreed to do so, although he recognised the dangers it posed to his own reputation. He also realised that their reputations too were at risk; for being a railwayman was a much sought after occupation within the working class. Thus he advised in his first talk, 'you'll be misunderstood in this town. Please do not resort to violence no matter how much people may tease you. Keep calm and the best thing is to keep yourselves occupied. Organise football matches, go to your gardens and join classes; industrial history or English. But whatever you do, you'll be misunderstood but keep your cool'.

This advice was very moderate and illustrated how much he himself was increasingly conscious of the conservative nature of the locality. It was almost as if he was speaking to himself! It was good advice and in the next few days he kept in regular contact with the strikers giving them talks and leading discussions. The General Strike was short-lived and after nine days most of the unions, including the railwaymen, returned to work. Only the miners remained out on strike. The local railwaymen had followed his advice and they remained his supporters on other issues in the future. But his support for them re-ignited opposition to himself.

Sometime later, the Director of Education revealed to the headmaster that, following the General Strike, he had received complaints from two county families who were demanding that the head should be disciplined. Their complaint was very straightforward and specific, 'That man Parrott, the new headmaster, he belongs to the Labour Party' and should be forced to resign from the party. The Director refused citing the fact that many other teachers in other parts of the county were office-holders in the Conservative Party only to be met by the response, 'Oh but that's different!'

He went on to say that he had received no complaints on a professional level from the inspectors, managers or parents of the school. Indeed, the general feeling was most complimentary towards Mr Parrott's educational initiatives. This support from the Director of Education was very important as Frank had chosen Kirkby Stephen specifically because another school, where he had been offered a post, had sought to limit his political activities and he simply was not prepared to accept that.

Throughout the remainder of the 1920s, he continued to develop his interests and share them with local inhabitants and in particular he encouraged the Old Scholars' Association to further develop its evening class programme.

This activity in turn led to the setting up of an active branch of the Workers' Educational Association in the town. The headmaster was a passionate believer in education throughout life and had been active in the WEA since a pupil teacher. Soon after he arrived in Kirkby Stephen he discovered to his delight that the first president of the WEA was Bishop Percival who had been born only a few miles away in Brough Sowerby. On 22 August 1903 the Bishop had been invited to chair the inaugural meeting of trade unionists and educationalists in Oxford to form 'an Association to promote Higher Education of Workingmen'. The headmaster immediately realised the saliency of this local link and wrote articles and letters to the local newspapers attempting to build on local pride.

Alongside these initiatives, he actively promoted his personal interests in international affairs and peace issues. His experiences during the war reinforced his religious beliefs, while embracing Quaker values made him even more determined to ensure that ordinary people understood the horrors of war and had an appreciation of international matters.

Partially with this work in mind, Frank took advantage of the school summer break to go on study tours to Geneva under the auspices of the Institute of International Relations in 1926, 1928 and 1929. Much of the activity was centred on the League of Nations Headquarters there. He had such high hopes for this inter-governmental organisation and on his return to Westmorland he gave numerous talks on these experiences and ideas.

In particular he had high hopes for young people whom he believed to be much more open-minded than older generations. He felt that the medium of drama was an especially good means for promoting the message. This he maintained had the dual advantage of getting across the messages to both actors and audiences. He wrote and published a number of one-act pageant plays. In 1926, he produced *Humanity Delivered*, the following year, *Disarmament*, and in 1931, *Recalling the Years* (Box 16, CAC). These were relatively popular and were produced across the United Kingdom, helping to spread a wider, popular understanding of international affairs.

Throughout Frank was still much involved in one of his other principal interests, domestic politics. The Labour Party nationally was beginning to flex its muscles once more having recovered from the disappointment of its minority government defeat in 1924. In the constituency of Westmorland, the local constituency party had spent the early- and mid-1920s extending and consolidating its membership which was concentrated in Kendal with smaller parties in Tebay and Windermere. The local Labour Party was formed at a meeting 'of a score or so of Labour men' in Kendal on 9 February 1921. The local weekly newspaper, The *Westmorland Gazette* (*WG*), mocked the initiative by using two quotes from the main instigator of the move, Cllr Thomas Watts. Apparently he had said on 29 January that, 'The time is not far distant, when Westmorland will have a Labour member in the House of Commons'. By 9 February he had become more circumspect and realistic when he said, 'In the dim and distant future, the time may come when we might have a man for Westmorland' (*WG*, 12 February 1921). At the time nothing else was reported in the local press of Labour's initiative probably because the county's political establishment were unsure of the possible attraction of the Labour Party.

Kendal was the largest town in the constituency with a considerable amount of industry, based principally on the manufacture of shoes, carpets, snuff, tobacco, turbines and a great deal of light engineering. The housing conditions in the town were appalling, amounting to little better than slums especially in the Fellside area of the town. The railway centre of Oxenholme was less than two miles from the town where a great deal of railway maintenance was carried out in addition to the housing of extra engines to supplement the trains travelling north to Scotland over the notorious Shap Summit. These industries demanded support from a plethora of smaller engineering works.

In the Kendal area, there had been socialist and labour supporters since before the end of the nineteenth century. The Rev. HV Mills had been elected one of Labour's earliest county councillors for the town in 1892 and there was a branch of the ILP formed in 1906 with members winning seats on local elected bodies.

Slightly further north, Tebay was a considerable railway junction with large engine sheds which also provided additional 'banker' engines for the trains as they journeyed up the main line over Shap Fell when the single engines were incapable of doing so. In addition, the LNER line from County Durham via Kirkby Stephen joined the main line at Tebay providing further demand for railway workers. The railway trade unions were active in Labour politics having moved the original motion at the Trades Unions Congress in 1899 to establish a political party independent of the two major parties. This led, in 1900, to the establishment of the Labour Representation Council which six years later became the Labour Party. These union members were active in establishing a Labour presence politically in the locality. In neighbouring Shap, a railway clerk, C C Poole, was much involved and in the 1935 General Election unsuccessfully contested Shrewsbury for the Labour cause.

The town of Windermere had only come into existence following the arrival of the railway in 1847. It was the terminus of the branch line but nevertheless did provide a number of railway servicing and maintenance jobs, in addition to the routine station posts. The area also had a number of engineering jobs in a factory nearby which produced machinery for the local bobbin making factories. In addition, in the early years of the twentieth century the area's beauty attracted artists and early environ-mentalists who often harboured socialist tendencies. The legacy of John Ruskin who lived in nearby Coniston still remained after his death in 1901. Ruskin's death prompted the Labour Party Leader, Keir Hardie MP to observe, 'Thus disappears from earthly view the last of the giants who made the modern British socialist movement possible' (*The Keir Hardie Calendar*, p.11). Ruskin's ideas were put into effect in the locality in the form of cottage-type industries, such as spinning and linen-manufacture. In Bowness on Windermere, Annie Garnett established a small factory which flourished for many years specialising in hand embroidery on Ruskin's principles and employing ninety at its peak. Although this may not have created collective solidarity, it did engender a notion of social-ism and provided respectability amongst the middle-class, artistic com-munity. A branch of the ILP was formed in the town in 1908 and was still functioning in 1924 (Clark, 2012 p.12).

With these districts as the base, and having been encouraged by the Labour Party's achievement of almost a third of the vote in a straight fight against the Conservative in 1924, the local Constituency Labour Party decided to contest the next election due in 1929. The Party was still weak across the constituency and drastically short of finance and cars but it had a network of members and an embryonic organisation. It had learned lessons from the 1924 election and many of the local officers were still in post and had the experience of having fought a general elec-tion. Frank Parrott was much involved in this and indeed was influential in the choice of the candidate.

Walter Bone was chosen to carry the Labour Party's standard in the General Election of 1929 and he proved to be very active, addressing meetings across the far-flung county constituency. The constituency party cleverly ensured that these public meetings were chaired by a local personage wherever possible. This was an astute move for it gave the rel-atively new party an identity within the local community. In Kirkby Stephen, the choice was obviously Frank Parrott who chaired the meet-ing in the Temperance Hall, providing further evidence that the headmaster was always prepared to publicly show his political colours. In addition to acting as chairman, Frank had to address the meeting for some time whilst waiting for the candidate to arrive from an earlier meeting in Appleby. On Walter Bone's arrival, the meeting became very heated with the *Westmorland Gazette* running the headline, 'Mr Bone's lively meeting in Kirkby Stephen'. Throughout all the election campaigns, the *Westmorland Gazette* was very hostile to Labour for daring to challenge their favoured party, the Conservatives. For example, throughout all the campaigns, the Labour candidates were described as 'socialists'. In 1924, it made great play of Labour's supposed links with Russia (*WG*, 18 and 26 May 1929).

As Frank later recalled,

> ...the Labour candidate was a friend of mine in the Friends' Ambulance Unit named Walter Bone. Walter had been in Africa for a time and I wrote and told him that I would help him as far as I could for I was studying for my inter-degree. But sure enough he wanted hospitality and I offered if you are ever in the constituency come to my house. Like me he was a vegetarian...Walter was a warden at an educational settlement in Scunthorpe. But I warned Walter that he was taking on a tough job but in spite of that he stuck to the job but he didn't like it. But he was a personal friend of mine so that went against me.

In a sense he was exactly the type of candidate Frank Parrott would have wished for; similar in background, beliefs, education and experience. But this view was not shared by the electorate of Westmorland. Unfortunately, Labour's relative success in the previous election had induced the Liberals to run a candidate for the first time since 1910 and they polled well attracting 38.3 per cent of the vote. In spite of a very energetic campaign, Labour's vote plummeted to a mere 12.1 per cent thus losing their deposit and coming third in the poll. Frank Parrott felt his reputation was damaged in some quarters by his participation in the election on Labour's behalf. Interestingly, he also observed how difficult it was to contest a large rural constituency with only one car when your opponents had scores of vehicles available to them. This was felt to be a real handicap by many party activists and for example at a public meet-

45

ing in nearby Shap, the chairman was complaining that they had no cars at all at their disposal. Elsewhere party supporters were urged to go to the polling stations in their opponent's cars!

Incidentally, whenever a suitable local chair could not be found, the chairman of the Constituency Labour Party, Harry Walker, performed the role. Harry Walker was a printer, active in his union nationally, the Typographical Association, and he went on to unsuccessfully contest Blackburn in 1935 before becoming MP for Rossendale in Lancashire in 1945. He was a close friend of Frank Parrott and being a Methodist lay preacher, they shared the view that religion was a basic tenet of their political beliefs. A further common interest was that they were both committed temperance workers.

Frank was deeply disappointed by Ramsay MacDonald's behaviour in resigning as Labour prime minister and forming the National Government in 1931. He had identified with MacDonald in his conversion to socialism as a young man. 'I liked MacDonald initially. He was a good man…and of course he was a conscientious objector. I didn't like his attitude on getting to power and going to visit the King…He let me down'.

Partly as a result of this general disappointment, the Labour Party in Westmorland did not contest the next election of 1931 which followed the defeat of the minority Labour Government and Ramsay MacDonald's defection. One minor consequence was that at least Frank Parrott had some time in which to rebuild his reputation and support. Although he remained active in helping to run a small Labour Party branch in Kirkby Stephen, no elections were contested along party lines. This was the tradition throughout the constituency and even in Kendal, the most promising political area for the Labour Party, it was not until 1935 that Labour made a concerted and coordinated campaign for seats on the Kendal Town Council under the party label.

The first half of the new decade was a period of consolidation for Frank Parrott. He continued with his initiatives in his school which were proving popular with pupils and parents alike. He expanded his many extra-curricula activities with sports days and walking trips for the youngsters up the local fells such as the Nine Standards or Wild Boar Fell. To many this provided a new dimension to the concept of schooling and education. The Old Students' Association went from strength to strength providing a continuity of support for Frank in addition to the intrinsic value it offered the community.

Throughout the 1930s, he remained involved in the sporting life of the town, was a rover scout, active in the county branch of the National Union of Teachers, gave talks to any group who invited him and carried on his activities with the WEA. He was involved in the temperance movement through the local Band of Hope, remained a member of the RSPCA and NSPCC, formed the Kirkby Stephen Allotments Society and was prominent locally and regionally in the Playing Fields Association. He even gave talks against blood sports such as hunting which to many in Westmorland was anathema but Frank Parrott was a man of principle and firmly held beliefs and eventually the local people came to appreciate and admire him for that.

There was however one initiative in these years which brought together many of his interests. Throughout his life he had been an ardent Christian. In his younger days he had attended the Methodist Chapel in Wellingborough later becoming a lay preacher. Even after he ceased to be a formal member of the Methodist Church he gave scores of talks, lectures and sermons at chapels in north Westmorland. But his experiences as a medical orderly in World War I had led him eventually in 1920 to begin the formal journey to become a member of the Society of Friends, a Quaker.

When he arrived at Kirkby Stephen he discovered that although there was no formal Friends' Meeting House, there were several individuals who shared his religious persuasion. In particular he found a new ally in Joseph Clampitt, a foreman at the railway sheds in the town. Initially they met in each other's houses or they rented rooms but soon began to search for permanent quarters. They raised money from local and regional sources and after many difficulties, purchased a building in 1929 for £425 and spent almost the same amount renovating it. The following year, they opened their own Kirkby Stephen Meeting House (Box 12, CAC).

The building was too large so they adapted part of it for community use, letting the upper floor to the local scout troop who in turn sub-let part of it to TocH. Before too long however, they vacated the building and the upper floor was then let to the Youth Hostels Association and it became the first youth hostel in the Lakeland Region in 1931 with the ubiquitous Frank Parrott as the part-time, voluntary warden. The youth hostel later moved and was turned into a cottage but the Meeting House remains to this day. Frank Parrott began a long involvement with the YHA becoming Lakeland President in 1953, a position he held for many years.

Reminiscing in 1978, Frank Parrott described the mid-1930s as the best period for the Labour Party in Kirkby Stephen, '...that was the best time, when the wife of a minister of religion named Short contested the 1935 election. I remember he left to go to Dundee but she was an amazing candidate'. At this time Mrs E V Short lived in Kendal where her husband was the Unitarian Minister. Prior to coming to Westmorland she had been active in the Labour cause at Oxford University becoming only the second woman to be elected secretary of the University Labour Club. Her husband's ministry then took them to Shrewsbury and Gainsborough. In the latter town, both husband and wife were elected on the town council as Labour councillors. It was an exciting election campaign and Mrs Short gained the highest ever Labour vote of over 10,000 or almost one third of the vote in a straight fight against the Conservative. The mere fact that she was the first and only woman candidate caused quite a stir in this rather backward political community and seventy-five years later her campaign was even referred to in a favourable manner by the *Westmorland Gazette* during its coverage in the 2010 General Election (Clark, 2012 pp.105-108).

One common factor in Labour's three election forays in the inter-war years was the link with the church. The candidate in 1924, Reg Burnett, was the son of a Church of England clergyman and he himself had undertaken two years of study for the ministry at Cambridge University before becoming involved in politics and drama. In 1929 Walter Bone had been very active in the Society of Friends. The husband of Mrs Evelyn Short was a Unitarian Minister and she too was involved in the church activities. At a local level, two regular chairmen and speakers at Labour public meetings in the 1920s and 1930s were Reverend Basil Viney of Kendal and the Reverend S Liberty of Helsington near Kendal. Frank Parrott felt very comfortable with this Christian Socialist approach for it was so much in accord with his own view of politics.

Following the relative success for the Labour Party, Frank Parrott not only continued with his many interests but also became sufficiently confident to put himself forward as a candidate for the Kirkby Stephen Parish Council in 1937 and was duly elected. He was to remain on the council for thirty-seven years without an election defeat, including twenty-one as chairman.

During the spring of 1937, Frank was approached by a railwayman from nearby Tebay, who was a Labour activist and magistrate, as to whether he would be interested in becoming a magistrate on the local bench. He expressed an interest and he later wrote,

> On 12 May 1937, Coronation Day, I received a confidential letter from the Clerk of the Lieutenancy intimating that the Lord Chancellor wished to receive certain assurances in the event of your being appointed a JP. I gave those assurances and on 26 May, I was informed my appointment has now been made public (Box 6, CAC).

It is interesting to note that even then with his position in the community having been so firmly established, there were still those who were suspicious of him. The key point however, was that these concerns were over-ruled and he was appointed to one of the most senior positions in the local society. As expected, he undertook his new responsibilities in a conscientious and diligent manner.

He was believed to be the first schoolmaster in Westmorland to be made a JP and his appointment at the early age of forty-six did cause some consternation but critically, the managers of his school offered congratulations and were most supportive. In 1950 he was appointed chairman of the Kirkby Stephen Bench, a position he held with distinction until 1965. As part of these duties, in 1953, he was appointed to represent the Westmorland Quarter Sessions on the Visiting Committee of Durham Prison, a role which he found most satisfying. He thus became very friendly with the Labour MP for Bishop Auckland, James Boyden, and this friendship continued long after Frank had ceased to be a magistrate.

Whilst he had been developing all these local activities, he had not neglected his international interests. In 1934, he had undertaken a study tour of Denmark under the auspices of the Society of Friends which was entitled 'No more war'. Perhaps even more significant, in July and August of 1938 he made a further visit to Geneva. On that occasion he attended the annual summer school of the International Labour Organisation which was held at the League of Nations and the principal theme of the school was 'the coming slump' (Box 3, CAC).

In the later years of the 1930s, Frank became increasingly aware of the dangers facing Europe and especially, through contacts in the Society of Friends, of the threats to Jews on mainland Europe. He was involved in correspondence with at least two Jewish families prior to the Second World War. Both Frank and his wife Barbara continued this correspondence with Edith Reismann for over ten years from 1939 (Box 4, CAC). Following the outbreak of war, he arranged, through the Quakers, to have a woman from mainland Europe, Helene Leopold, staying in Kirkby Stephen with him and his wife. Presumably she was an internee of some description for Frank wrote to the Registration Officer on 25 November 1940 seeking permission for her to accompany himself and Mrs Parrott to a social event in Kendal one evening. He went on to explain she had not been out of the house for many weeks (Box 12, CAC). To have a woman from continental Europe staying with you in Kirkby Stephen during the war must have risked inviting hostile comment but this was another example of Frank Parrott standing up for his beliefs and principles.

Frank clearly saw the Second World War differently from how he had viewed the earlier conflict when he had refused to fight. On this occasion he was too old to enlist but he saw the evil of fascism confronting the world and supported the Allies efforts to defeat the threat. After the War, from 1947 to 1959, he corresponded with a German prisoner of war who had been in Featherstone POW Camp over the Pennines near Haltwhistle in Northumberland (Box 4, CAC). This illustrates his belief that one should not hold every German responsible for the actions of the Nazi State which was not exactly a popular position to hold in post-war England yet in accord with his strong Christian beliefs.

Interestingly, amongst the papers left by Frank Parrott is a horde of letters sent to him during the war by his former pupils at Kirkby Stephen Council School who were serving in the British Forces in many parts of the world. Subject of course to the censor's pen they give some picture of the life of ordinary service men and women. The real significance is the mere existence of these letters. The fact that so many felt such an allegiance to their former headmaster that, even in times of greatest stress and fear, they felt moved to correspondence with him is truly remarkable. He always was able to form a bond with young people by treating them as grown-ups. In school notes left by pupils in the 1930s are comments such as; 'Mr Parrott told us about the importance of elections' and 'Mr Parrott told us about the League of Nations' (Box 6, CAC).

Following the outbreak of the Second World War in 1939, the pressure on the headmaster intensified when school children from areas subjected to German bombing began to arrive in Kirkby Stephen. Initially they came from Newcastle and South Shields on Tyneside, then in May 1941, more evacuees began to arrive from Barrow in Furness on the west coast. Pressure on space became intense and every suitable room was commandeered. In Frank's words,

> We used the Temperance Hall, classrooms at the Centenary Methodist and Baptist Churches and the Friends' Meeting House. I well remember taking ninety-one children and seven teachers to the Nine Standards on a sunny afternoon in September. We ran a club in the Methodist Church for our evacuees. We also had many interesting entertainments and a canteen was opened in the Temperance Hall.

Throughout his life, Frank maintained an on-going interest in education and during the war years this dominated so much of his thinking. He was conscious of the opportunities that peace could bring in this sphere. Having been headmaster for fifteen years and with a number of successes to his name, he was an established and respected figure in the county's educational establishment. Furthermore, he was prominent in the National Union of Teachers. At various times in his career he was both the district and the county president of the National Union of Teachers. He realised that following victory, the men returning home, as well as the population in general, would demand great changes in education.

In 1942 confidence of victory was beginning to emerge and the government was turning its attention to reconstruction after the war. Lord Beveridge's Report into the social fabric of Britain encompassed social benefits, pensions and education. In the autumn of 1942, the

Westmorland County Council organised a high level consultative conference in Langdale in the centre of the Lake District and Frank was very
much involved. In turn this was to feed into work being undertaken by
the Labour MP, J Chuter Ede, who was the junior education minister in
the coalition government. Eventually, this was enacted under Rab Butler
MP as the Education Act of 1944. This Act revolutionised the English
educational system including making provision for secondary schooling
for all. Until then, most pupils stayed on at the junior schools, until they
were fourteen and, in the case of Kirkby Stephen's Council School and
others like it, that remained the position until April 1955.

Frank Parrott was overjoyed with the result of the General Election of
July 1945 which brought in a Labour Government with a majority of 146
over all the other parties. He had thought that the British people might
take the opportunity after the horrors of the war to vote for a massive
change and this they did. He had high expectations and was generally
delighted with the progress under Clement Attlee's Government.

In Westmorland he was involved in supporting the Labour candidate
who on this occasion was an unusual choice, with Captain H B
Richardson being the standard bearer. He had served in the Ghurka
Rifles during the war and prior to that had spent ten years in India, for a
period as Education Minister in Indore State (*WG*, 23 June 1945). Again
he was clearly a man with whom Frank had common interests.
Predictably, although attracting over nine thousand votes, he was only
second in a four-cornered contest. Frank however, did have the consola-
tion of seeing his old friend Harry Walker from Kendal being elected MP
for Rossendale.

With the end of hostilities, and the general election behind him, Frank
Parrott picked up the other issues he had espoused in the pre-war days.
He reinvigorated the Workers' Educational Association in the Kirkby
Stephen district becoming its chairman and always prepared to give lec-
tures under its auspices. A little later he formed a local branch of the
United Nations' Association and continued the work he had undertaken
under the old League of Nations. He remained active in the local Vale of
Eden Band of Hope (the temperance body) and was much involved in
the Youth Hostels Association; being elected the Lakeland Regional
President in 1953, whilst he pursued his interests in the Playing Fields'
Association.

In April 1946, he successfully stood for the Kirkby Stephen Ward of North Westmorland Rural District Council, which he held for twenty-one years and six elections, until his retirement in 1967. Then on 30 December 1953, Frank Parrott retired from the Council School after twenty-eight years as headmaster at the age of sixty-three. It was a far cry from the days following his arrival in Kirkby Stephen. In 1925, he was regarded with suspicion if not hostility as 'the man who took the *Daily Herald* and who is in the Labour Party'. He was now an established figure in the community and was highly regarded throughout North Westmorland.

Frank Parrott in later life (as local councillor)

Following his retirement, Frank found more time to devote to his many other interests. He had to leave his school house and he moved the short distance to Brougham House in the centre of Kirkby Stephen. He was in great demand as a speaker at numerous groups across Cumbria. He was the unpaid correspondent to both the local weekly papers, the *Cumberland and Westmorland Herald* and the *Westmorland Gazette*. He was now unchallenged as a pillar of the local community.

In the late summer of 1957, the county councillor for Kirkby Stephen died and in October, Frank successfully stood for the vacant position. On Westmorland County Council he immediately aligned himself with the Labour Group and in particular was at the centre of their efforts to introduce comprehensive education across the county. There had been comprehensive schools since the end of the Second World War, where the sparse population in the rural communities made tri-partite secondary education impractical. The long established Windermere Grammar School became the first comprehensive school in England to which all boys in the area at the age of eleven were admitted, whilst later a similar reorganisation occurred in North Westmorland. But in spite of this situation, the Labour Group's efforts proved to be in vain and it was only with the creation of Cumbria County Council in 1974 that Frank was to see his cherished comprehensive scheme become a reality.

His service to the community was officially recognised in 1965 when he was awarded an OBE. Frank raised the possibility that he might be offered the award with the local Labour Party branch where he was urged to accept as 'no local Conservative has ever had such an award'.

The following year, one of his long time friends and supporters, Jonathan (Jonty) Burton was selected to become Lord Mayor of Newcastle upon Tyne. He had originally been a railwayman in Kirkby Stephen and a disciple of Frank but in 1939 had been transferred to Tyneside where he had become active in the Labour Party with great success. He was the agent for the local MP and cabinet minister, the Rt Hon. Ted Short, who also had originally come from Orton not far from Kirkby Stephen. Frank Parrott had the honour of being the speaker at the Lord Mayor's Dinner.

In 1967 at the age of seventy-six, perhaps the first signs were seen of Frank's retrenchment from formal public affairs when he retired from the local rural district council. He retained his other interests and in March 1972 was elected as an Alderman on Westmorland County Council. This was a prestigious position which in essence meant that he remained on the council without having to contest elections. Only the senior and most respected councillors were accorded this honour.

The following May, he suffered the sad loss of his wife of fifty-four years, Barbara. They had shared many common interests including political beliefs, both being long-time members of the Labour Party. In particular, in York the couple had campaigned in their younger days for women's suffrage. From the time when he was converted to socialism, Frank had believed in this cause and throughout his political career he campaigned for the rights of women. Not surprisingly, Barbara's death left Frank devastated and a couple of years later he stood down as chair of the parish council although remaining a member until it disappeared under local government reorganisation in 1974. In the same year, Westmorland County Council also disappeared and Frank's last remaining public office finished.

But he still retained his active interests in a host of voluntary bodies. When the Settle to Carlisle railway line was threatened with closure in 1983, one of the first to launch the campaign to save it, was the nonagenarian, Frank Parrott. A few years earlier, he had also begun an annual sponsored walk for local charities which he continued until his death on 29 July 1986, aged ninety-five.

Frank Parrott lived a remarkable life. He showed it was possible to achieve success in the local community as a socialist even in the most unpromising environment such as Kirkby Stephen had been when he first arrived in 1925. At that time he was met by prejudice but by living according to his high standards he eventually became recognised for the man that he was. As the local headmaster, he undoubtedly had some status in the town and as such he was able gradually to build a rapport with his pupils and their parents. Over the years, he truly became a pillar of the society. He had so much energy and his interests were so wide that little happened in Kirkby Stephen in which he was not involved.

He had met such suspicion, bordering on hostility, when he first arrived but even in this most inauspicious environment, he never attempted to hide his socialist beliefs. His form of socialism, which was largely of an ethical nature, was in a sense well-suited to the district which had a long-established nonconformist religious tradition and it did find a responsive chord. Early on he had made an assessment of the position in North Westmorland and decided that progress would be gradual and that he would have first to gain the confidence of the local people. He set out to do this and once achieved, the people did not let him down. He was never defeated in any elections; parish, district or county. Indeed he almost always topped the poll.

He acknowledged his successful strategy in an interview in 1978 when, aged eighty-eight, he commented, 'I think if I had stayed on to live in

York or Wellingborough, my socialist activities would have been more strongly developed than here. We are out on a limb here…But I would not have had it otherwise'.

When nearly ninety, he was invited to comment on the modern Labour Party; he reiterated his faith in the organisation saying,

> I do feel, something I wish that I could recapture, the enthusiasm and ideas of the early pioneers. I wish they could inject a sense of 'worthwhileness' from the point of view of ethical standards. I do know that enthusiasm and almost religious fervour does exist in some quarters and that gives me hope and encouragement.

More than a quarter of a century after his death, older members of the community in the Kirkby Stephen district still recalled Frank Parrott and the constant refrain is, 'He was a really good man'.

Quotations of Frank W Parrott from interviews with David Clark on 17 January 1978 and 27 October 1978.

3

Tess Nally
1895-1988

Teresa Veronica Nally (nee Mullen), or Tess as she preferred to be called, was born on 3 January 1895 at Shevington, near Wigan. She was the middle child of thirteen of a mining family. From this inauspicious background she was to hold together quite a Labour dynasty in the North West of England later in the twentieth century.

Her husband Tom, became leader of Manchester City Council whilst being employed as a Co-operative Party agent. Their son Will, was the Labour MP for Bilston in Staffordshire and twin daughters, Alice and Winifred (Win) were active in the movement in both South Lancashire and across the Pennines in West Yorkshire.

Her early childhood experiences had a lasting effect on her and especially the size of the families in her community which inevitably aggravated the poverty. As she described over 75 years later, her parents, 'were very poor and always trying to make ends meet and wondering what to do. It really was terrible for a man and his wife to bring up in those days a family of children. I never remember having a new frock. Everything was handed down and so on'.

The grinding poverty was in spite of the fact that her father worked at the local pit. From an early age the poverty which she so associated with large families influenced her attitude towards Roman Catholicism? She couldn't understand why her mother, already so hard pressed bringing up so many children and managing a miner's house, regarded it as such an honour to wash the priest's blankets or that she kept a bottle of whisky in the house just for him. She even disliked her name Teresa as 'it was too catholic', preferring to be called Tess.

The most abiding reason for Tess's developing opinions was simply that she saw her mother and the neighbours having more children than they could cope with (Wheable-Archer, 2010 p.18). Later that led to her being deeply involved in the birth control movement for which she campaigned for the rest of her life. After leaving home, she completely rejected Roman Catholicism and repeatedly resisted pressure to return to the faith.

When she left home she found work a few miles away in an uncle's public house in the colliery village of Astley, near Leigh. It was whilst working there, she met her future husband Tom Nally, who worked in the coal mines. He too had an Irish father but an Orangeman from Northern Ireland. Tom was a very bright young man who was attending night school at Leigh Technical College with the aim of entering the management in the mines. She was captivated by the young man who was intelligent, enjoyed reading and had exciting ideas on how society should be changed to reduce poverty and give everyone a fair chance. They married in the Church of England's, St Stephen's at Astley on 3 June 1914.

Tom's father, William, worked in the local pits all his life and was active in the local branch of the miners' union. He was self-educated and devoted considerable time in teaching his fellow miners to read and take an interest in events around them. Like many working men of the age he was keen that Tom, whom he regarded as bright, 'improved' himself by obtaining qualifications which would enhance his opportunities in life. At a relatively young age, Tom achieved the necessary certificates and became an undermanager at the Nook Mine employing 200 men. Interestingly, he was in charge of his father and brothers which, although potentially a source of conflict, did mean that he was constantly aware of the conditions and feelings of the ordinary miners. His position also meant that on his marriage to Tess, they moved into a thirteen-roomed company house near the pithead.

During World War I, the demand for coal was great and the miners received slightly better pay and conditions than in the pre-war days. However as the war drew to a close these advances were threatened and then reversed. Tom was infuriated by the actions of the mine owners and resigned from management. He decided he would return to the coal face as an ordinary miner and fight for better conditions.

At that time, opportunities occurred for miners from the traditional coalfields to work in the more productive Nottinghamshire mines and in 1919, Tom and Tess decided to move. He found work in Gedling Pit and lived in digs until he could find accommodation for Tess and their son Will, who had been born in Astley on 15 December 1914. It didn't take Tom long to find accommodation for his young family who moved into a three-bedroomed terrace house in Godfrey Street, Netherfield. This was a strongly working-class community, largely of miners and railway workers and the Nally family quickly fitted in. On 30 September 1919, the family increased with the birth of the twins, Alice and Winifred, who as one would have expected were 'named' in the Socialist Sunday School.

Tom, with Tess' encouragement, threw himself into trade union work and Labour politics with great enthusiasm. The couple remained initially members of the ILP but also took advantage of the new rules for individual membership of the Labour Party and joined. Their commitment to the Socialist Sunday School was strong and the family remained active in the movement.

The three siblings of the Nally family were growing up under the watchful guidance of Tess. Both Tom and Tess became members of the local co-op committee and they all attended the Socialist Sunday School. In addition, Tom was elected as a Labour councillor on Carlton Urban District Council.

At work he immediately began to pursue an active role in the Nottinghamshire Miners' Association (NMA) which was regarded as one of the weaker bodies in the Miners' Federation of Great Britain (MFGB). It was a particularly difficult time in the NMA as serious tensions were emerging within it. The President, George Spencer, was having disagreements with other regional leaders in the MFGB. He had become President of the NMA in 1912 and during World War I, campaigned with a Liberal MP to abolish the NMA's political fund. Then in 1918 he became General Secretary of the NMA and in December 1918 was elected as the Labour MP for Broxtowe in the county but even then continued as somewhat of a maverick with very eclectic views.

These were turbulent times in Nottingham mining politics. Added to the unrest amongst miners over wage cuts, the dissension encouraged by George Spencer exacerbated the woes. Tom never had any hesitation about which side he was on and throughout argued for the miners to remain united in one organisation. He remained unstintingly loyal to the Nottinghamshire Miners' Association. With Tess's full support he continued his campaigning for the NMA through the 1921 strike and 1926 General Strike. He travelled widely throughout the county becoming one of the recognised leaders of the rank and file miners and constantly arguing for unity.

But the situation in the mining industry across the country was worsening with the mine owners determined to keep their profits high through wage cuts and increased hours. The miners naturally were equally determined to protect their living standards, low as they might be. Eventually, the Government realised that action had to be taken with the country being completely dependent upon coal. Nationally, in these years there were more than one and a quarter million miners.

The Government appointed the Samuel Commission to examine the situation and it reported on 10 March 1926. Meanwhile the coal owners had announced a lockout of miners beginning on 1 May. Initially, the Prime Minister, Stanley Baldwin attempted to broker a settlement on the basis of the Samuel Report but it proved impossible largely due to the intransigence of the mine owners who were still insisting on wage cuts, longer hours and district wage bargaining.

On the other hand the miners were united in refusing to accept these conditions. They determined to fight under the evocative slogan, 'Not a penny off the pay, not a second on the day'. There was complete unity amongst the rank and file miners and even in Nottinghamshire there was one hundred percent backing for the fight.

The MFGB and the TUC joined forces and called a General Strike beginning on 4 May. The response was tremendous but the Government had prepared their ground carefully with huge stockpiles of coal ready to meet the nation's demands. After 9 days the TUC called off the General Strike leaving the miners locked out for a further seven months.

Then came a bitter time for the miners and their families. Many miners were shocked that they had been left alone but fought on. For over three months, there was little dissension as they struggled on, with conditions worsening every day.

A contemporary of Tom's and stalwart of the NMA, Bernard Taylor, who later became Labour MP for Mansfield and a Life Peer, described in an honest and straightforward manner the situation in Nottinghamshire at the end of September 1926,

> The moment had arrived when a determined effort was being made to sow the seeds of dissension in the ranks, and break the strike; and in Nottinghamshire it produced results. The circumstances of semi-starvation, the fear among the men that their jobs would be taken, and the prospect of victimization and unemployment were strings pulling at their hearts, and the position worsened daily. Nottinghamshire was regarded in other parts of the coalfield as a black spot and the weakest link in the chain of the Miners' Federation of Great Britain. It was all too obvious by October that the battle was lost as far as Nottinghamshire was concerned. But there were pockets of resistance in every part of the county composed of men who said they were not prepared to bow the knee to Baal and to forsake the Miners' Federation (Taylor, 1972 p.40).

The position in the county had been made more difficult and divisive when on 5 October at a mass meeting, the men at the Digby and New London pits decided to return to work. What was significant was that the NMA's General Secretary, George Spencer, was present and on behalf of the men managed to reach an agreement with the coal owners for the miners to return to work. He then went on to make further agreements at other pits. The MFGB was furious and summoned Spencer, who refused to apologise and was suspended from the MFGB.

Spencer was expelled from the Labour Party and sat for the remainder of the Parliament with the Liberals. He went on to form his own separate union, the Nottingham and District Miners' Industrial Union, which had the overt support of the coal owners. Eventually it spread from Nottinghamshire to most of the other coalfields although its strength was always in the Dukeries. It however weakened the MFGB in the aftermath of the General Strike defeat and caused bitter divisions in the mining communities. The coal owners would only recognise Spencer's union and the NMA struggled to survive. It was only due to the loyalty of some rank and file members and leaders such as Tom Nally and Bernard Taylor that it did. It was not until 1937 that a merger of the two unions took place with Spencer returning as President of the NMA!

Although approximately a quarter of the miners across the country were driven back to work by the end of October, the majority of the rank and file remained resolute against capitulating. However by the end of November, the Government was importing vast quantities of coal and the transport workers and seamen were unable to stop these imports. The money being paid to the strikers by the unions was rapidly drying up and after a series of conferences and ballots, the MFGB entered into talks with the Government and on 29 November, recommended a return to work. It was a humiliating defeat and left bitterness in the mining communities for decades.

The defeat of the miners, one of the most effectively organised unions, led to a great deal of heart-searching about the means by which working people could achieve their political ambitions. Following the Bolshevik Revolution in Russia in 1917, there had been a school of thought that political objectives could be achieved through industrial action. The defeat of the miners and the collapse of the General Strike after a mere nine days, forced many to re-assess their position. The Labour Party had massively increased its share of the vote and its seats in Parliament since 1910 and had even formed a minority Government at Westminster in 1923. Tom Nally and Bernard Taylor were just two of many who were to refocus their fight for the rights of working people through political means.

As in most coal disputes, the miners' wives played a crucial role in supporting their husbands and families and never more so than in 1926. Tess was one of those wives. Not only did she provide unstinting support for Tom, running the house, looking after their three children but also working within the wider mining community. She describes graphically those days,

> We had a shed at the back of our house in Nottingham (backing onto a railway line) and I heard that Marion Phillips (National Womans Officer of the Labour Party) could get leather soles and heels and she sent bags. I sent her the address where to send them…She sent the leather soles and heels, cut out, and bags of clothes. Some were good and some were finery; a princess should have worn them. Lacy dresses and all that sort of thing were no use to miners' wives. Odd socks, spats galore, bags and bags of it

came. Top hats that can flatten, I used to laugh you know, every time diving into this bag to see what was in it. I used to tip it in the yard usually because I didn't know where it had come from and we found all these sorts of things which was very funny.

Although she recalled the amusing side of the experience fifty years later she was eternally grateful for people's generosity at the time, explaining away the eccentricities by the donors' lack of knowledge about the conditions in which miners lived,

> They hadn't the slightest idea, they had never been in a mining village or talked to a miner. They had no idea of the life they led or the wages they got, or the cottages or anything; no baths, no hot water. You had to carry your (tin) bath onto the rug. The kids used to go out and you'd bathe. In the older cottages that was the only way the men bathed and then the opposition used to say, 'Oh they'll only put it in the bath, you know'.

They were such bitter times and Tess describes how this once drove her to actions she always regretted. The Nallys' garden shed became a cobbler's shop which families used to visit for assistance. Tess described one incident,

> One of the mistakes of my life which I will never forget is that two little boys came, oh with terrible shoes and I sent them back. I wouldn't let these two men mend them because their father had gone back to work. Now that was the wrong thing for me to do. I should not have done it but we were so bitter. They were being treated by everybody, the grocers and everybody else, miners and all the rest of them. That was how I felt and I have always said I should not have sent those boys back. I mean those little boys because it wasn't their fault. But that they had broken away, they had been blacklegging, they had been working a fortnight you see. So that was the reason. Their dad was a very nice railwayman. I always think about this. Not a J H Thomas type (the General Secretary of National Union of Railwaymen).

That incident forever haunted Tess. Many of the railway men remained supporters of the miners although their union had decided to return to work. As the trains passed along the line adjoining the Nallys' garden some of the drivers would throw lumps of coal onto the line-side.

> They used to throw these little lumps of coal over onto the line and we couldn't carry them. And we'd get the lads, the bigger lads, and they would carry them. I used to think that's doing them one in the eye.

The solidarity of working-class communities ensured that some of the miners' hardship was mitigated whenever possible. One of the daughters, Win, who wrote an excellent autobiography, recalled, going with her father to collect his strike pay and seeing the miners, having collected their own meagre monies, giving some of it to help support those miners who were locked out but were not union members (Wheable-Archer, 2010 p.17).

Tess also provided a lead in establishing soup kitchens. Both she and Tom were on the committee of the Netherfield Co-operative Society and she describes her approach to,

> the head butcher of Netherfield Co-operative. Well I went to him one morning and said to him, 'Well what about it George, haven't you got some spare bones?' He said, 'What for?' 'Well', I said, 'they're talking about opening a soup kitchen because things are very, very bad'. And he said, 'Well yes, you can have my boiler house'. He had a boiler house at the back of where he used to boil pigs' feet and that. So of course, he used to give them the best bones with meat on.

Win recalls that their kitchen in effect became a shop. Arrangements were made with the local Co-op to supply staple foodstuffs. She remembers large tins of cocoa, dried milk powder and long loaves and how she and her twin sister Alice, used to love helping in the 'shop' (Wheable-Archer, 2010 p.16).

There was widespread support in the local communities for the miners' families with church groups, railwaymens' wives as well as the local

Labour Parties playing their part. Throughout the country constituency Labour Parties rallied round raising money. Even in rural Westmorland for example, over £313 (£16,675 in 2014 values) was raised for the miners; a not an insignificant amount from people who themselves were badly paid (Clark, 2012 p.93).

In order to relieve the pressure on the parents, a scheme was launched in London, largely through Labour Party members to take miners' children and look after them for the duration of the lockout - wartime evacuation in reverse. Tess felt this was a worthwhile venture which ought to be supported.

In fact she had already come to a similar private arrangement for the two girls to go and live in Chesham, Buckinghamshire with Labour Party friends, Amy and Wilf Cook. Win wrote later what a fascinating experience it was for her, exploring the countryside and watching the animals and birds. She also recalls being taken to listen to a Welsh miners' male voice choir which visited the area to raise funds for the strikers and how the crowd made a fuss of the twins when it was discovered they were miners' children (Wheable-Archer, 2010 p.17).

Initially when Tess approached other mothers, she was met with blank refusals. It wasn't until she entered her own son's name that others finally joined as well.

> They got this scheme and I went round asking the mothers would they allow their son or daughter to go. They had to be a certain age and mothers gave their luncheons. And I said my son's going, Will's going. He didn't want to go of course but I said, 'He's going. They'll be all right. They'll all be all right. There'll be fifty of you'. We took fifty down to Euston Station. They all stood in line and these mothers were waiting. Some of them, they wouldn't like at all. They were entirely different but they were kind and I thought it was a good thing that they had offered to open their home to a miner's child without knowing anything about them which they obviously didn't. When Will opened his case they said was he sure he was a miner's son because his clothes were clean and that sort of thing.

The scheme wasn't a complete success and a number of children soon returned home although others made lasting friendships. It was however an example of the sympathy to, and support for, the miners. Much of this was again organised through local branches of the Labour Party and trade unions although there was wider support.

When the lockout ended on the 29 November, there was a fear that most of the union activists would not be taken back but there was such a demand for coal and miners, that most, including Tom were taken back. Tom's actions during the dispute had made a favourable impression on his fellow workmates for he was soon elected as the checkweighman at the pit. This was an important role for he acted as the miners' representative when the amount of coal hewed was measured for the calculation of their wages. Checkweighmen were not paid by the mine owners but by the miners at the coal face. Only the most respected and trustworthy were elected to these positions.

Nationally, the Government wasted no time and pushed through the Trades Disputes and Trade Union Act of 1927 which made it even more difficult for unions to become involved in industrial disputes and for them to provide financial help to the Labour Party. The mine owners and their government ensured that they got their pound of flesh and then rubbed the workers noses in it.

With the emergence of the Spencer Union, Nottinghamshire became a battleground between conflicting groups of miners and Tom Nally and his family were in the thick of it. Tom worked hard at Gedling Pit as checkweighman whilst continuing to travel around the county and wider on NMA business, making friends as he did so. Most of these journeys he made on his bicycle, with Tess continuing with her work with the Co-operative movement. Later in 1927, the family moved a short distance to a new semi-detached house in Frederick Avenue, Carlton Hill.

It was in these formative years that Will, Winifred and Alice imbibed the spirit of socialism which remained with them for the rest of their lives. In their own way, each of them carried those socialist beliefs into practice in Parliament, local government and the magistracy. Socialism became their religion with a new trinity; the Labour Party, the Trade Union and the Co-operative.

Nottingham was the frontline in the struggle between the MFGB and the Spencer Union. Miners' leaders from other districts descended on the County to help the campaign. In spring 1928, the General Secretary of the MFGB, A J Cook, alongside other miners' leaders, S O Davies and Arthur Horner spent several weeks in the county (Arnot, 1953 p.537). A J Cook, who Tom knew well, stayed with the Nallys.

On 6 March 1928, the Nottingham County Council Elections were held and the miners were determined to use the secret ballot to express their views. There were a number of successes for Labour, including Tom Nally in the Kimberley-Eastwood Ward. Tom's campaign became a cause celebre in the county. He had the effrontery to stand against Colonel Sir Dennis Readett-Bayley, a long standing county councillor, but even more symbolically, the Chairman of Digby Colliery Company and thus Tom's employer.

On the day when nominations for the election closed, Tom went into work as normal to find, stuffed into his miner's lamp, a note from the management, saying his services were no longer required. Colonel Sir Dennis had sacked Tom for having the effrontery to stand against him. As the news spread, working people in the community were shocked and a bitter county council election ensued. It was described as 'the County Council Election of the Century' and the local newspaper ran the head-line, 'Clear Class Issues'.

Naturally, Tess was much involved and traipsed up and down the ward campaigning. She was a very trim woman, although never having much money, just knew how to look presentable and smart. In these days, local Labour campaigns did not have access to motor cars which the Conservatives normally had in numbers. Tess decided to redress the imbalance and hatched a plan to take Labour voters to the polls in the Tory cars. She described the incident which was only really possible because of her respectable appearance,

> The miners' wives came out and they had never fought any elec-tions (Sir D Bayley had usually been elected unopposed) so they'd no idea. And this lovely car and these drivers and they were all lined up in a row. Well I was pretty respectable and I lived away from Kimberley, so I went across and said, 'Excuse me, I would like to help if you would allow me to' and Lady Bayley said she was delighted. So I took one of these blinking cars and took it all round the streets. I said, 'Now you've not to look at our committee rooms!' So I went with them and packed them all in and they came.

They made such a fuss 'cos they'd never had an election. It was a wonderful thing for them you know. I will always remember that.

When I was running in and out of the Tory headquarters, Lady Bayley said, 'It's a very good job I brought quite a selection of white gloves' because these miners' wives were shaking hands with her. They were getting all black. She was getting shocked. Anyway we were all delighted and I was making a fuss of them all. 'Oh I hope Sir Dennis would get back' and all the rest of it. They didn't know who I was of course because I didn't live in the village. But it wasn't a very nice thing to do but still I thought, 'Oh well it's the survival of the fittest'.

On 6 March the results vindicated Tom's bravery with a victory,

Tom Nally (Labour)	1181
Sir H Dennis Bayley (Coal owner)	815

In his victory address, Tom said it was a triumph for A J Cook and a defeat for all his enemies whether in the Labour movement or outside. Two weeks later, Cook spoke to a large crowd of supporters in Hucknall Market Place and thanked all those who had helped Labour win in the recent county council elections (Nottinghamshire NUM Area History, internet p.10).

Tom however had lost his job.

Throughout all the turmoil of the lockout, and Tom's struggle on behalf of the NMA, Tess was nurturing another dream; that of establishing a branch of the Birth Control Movement in the county. She had felt passionately about the issue primarily as a result of what she had seen as a child in Lancashire and her rejection of Roman Catholicism.

Tess never returned to religion. As she was later to explain,

Quite frankly, I am a free thinker and until I have proof, I don't believe in all of this, because there wouldn't be so much wickedness if God could help...; It makes you think. I see people and I tell them, I don't need religion.

The move to the new house in 1927 at nearby Carlton Hill gave her the opportunity to turn her dream into reality and she established the first birth control clinic in Nottinghamshire which led to much vilification in the local press and amongst some individuals. Tess however felt so strongly but realised it would be even more effective to have a clinic in the City of Nottingham.

She set about finding premises and for weeks trailed around the City streets with a twin on each arm, exemplifying she felt her love of children, until she finally persuaded a Polish émigré tailor to let her have the use of the upper floor of his house for her weekly clinic. It wasn't the most popular move and the tailor lost some business whilst Tom as a county councillor had to defend his wife on numerous occasions. In these days, it was pioneering work and the official policy of the Birth Control Movement was only to assist married women although Tess and her committee members ignored this. They helped all who sought assistance (Wheable-Archer, 2010 p.18).

Following his sacking from the Gedling Mine, Tom went from pit to pit in search of work but to no avail. He was by now well-known, regarded as a trouble maker and on the employers' blacklist. There was no work for him in the pits.

He was offered a job in Nottingham with the Russian Oil Company but he wouldn't accept the condition of making donations to the Communist Party. Then the Nottingham Co-operative Society came to his rescue and provided him with some work developing 'mutuality clubs' for members and he also became the part-time Parliamentary agent for the Rushcliffe Constituency. This, with his local and county council work kept Tom busy, but he knew he had to find something more permanent. Not an easy task in the midst of a world depression, with mass unemployment in Britain. It was even more challenging when it is appreciated that the industry in which he was qualified to work, was closed to him on account of his being on the coal owners' blacklist.

Tess explained how the situation changed,

> So he picked up the paper one morning, the *Co-op News* we used to get, and he saw an advert for a co-op secretary. He said, 'I think I'll have a go at this Tess'. I said, 'You have no chance, no possible chance'. But he says, 'Well. I'll have a go'. Because his mother lived very near and he says, 'Well I'll have a day off anyhow. I'll go'. So

of course he wrote, got an interview and he went. There were so many of the other gang voting for their own chaps that Tom slipped in and he got the secretary of the Co-operative Party in Manchester and we had Gibson for an MP.

They were reluctant to leave their new house in Nottinghamshire but realised it was inevitable. Tom appreciated that his approach to politics had shifted following the failure of the General Strike. A Labour Government had been elected again in 1929 and the way forward seemed to be through political means in Parliament and local government.

But he had made a big impression and many friends. One such person was Tom Williams MP who had been elected for Don Valley in south Yorkshire in November 1922 and was to become Labour's most successful Minister of Agriculture. In his autobiography he wrote of Tom Nally during that desperate period following the General Strike,

> At one pit, where my old friend Tom Nally had arranged for me to speak, most of the men had already gone back; we were warned off the premises. Not to be defeated (defeat and Tom Nally hardly went together), we made a tactical withdrawal to the nearby railway station from which the men would soon be catching the train home. I spoke to the men until the train came in, then I sprinted off the platform as I had no ticket. In a situation like that one, mingling humiliation and excitement, Tom Nally was a good man to have beside you. He knew all the dangers and faced them….He was a great character and as true as steel (Williams, 1965 p.72).

In April 1930, Tom was chosen from 158 applicants to become secretary of the Manchester and District Co-operative Party (M & D) and the Parliamentary Agent for H M Gibson, who was Labour and Co-operative MP for Mossley in Greater Manchester.

Herbert M Gibson was born in 1896, the youngest of five and been brought up in poverty. On leaving school he became an office boy in the Town Hall at Manchester and was active in the co-operative movement, studying politics and economics at the Co-operative College, in the city.

Gibson won Mossley in May 1929 by 5029 votes, only to lose it two years later in the Labour debacle He was never to return to Parliament but had an illustrious career in the co-operative movement, ending up as a director of the Co-operative Wholesale Society.

The Nally family uprooted and moved north to live in 100 Denton Road, Audenshaw, whilst Tom's work office was provided by the Droylsden Co-operative Society at Edge Lane.

He was to described his work in the constituency succinctly,

> The policy pursued by the Mossley Division after Mr Gibson's election was a wise one. The activities of the agent, in addition to routine political organisation, were directed largely to the welfare of electors within the Division. Local parties utilized to the full the services of the agent in unemployment and rent cases, and a large number of cases were brought to a successful conclusion (Nally, 1939 p.11).

Suddenly, Tom's careful planning for Herbert Gibson's next election campaign was thrown into disarray. The minority Labour Government of 1929 was wrestling with the interminable problem of the world depression against the background of a demand for cuts in public spending at home. Eventually in the Summer of 1931 Ramsay MacDonald, the Labour Prime Minister, was persuaded to form a National Government with a small number of Labour MPs leaving with him, including Philip Snowden and J H Thomas. Labour was decimated at the polls with the number of its MPs falling from 257 to 52. Herbert Gibson, although polling reasonably well in Mossley, was one of the losers. This left a bitter taste with most Labour party members throughout the country.

In 1939, Tom perceptively described the local position,

> October, 1931 saw the Party fighting again in the Mossley Division when on a wave of fear and ignorance amongst the electors, plus the gross betrayal of Labour by leaders to whom the Party had for too long given confidence. Working-class candidates went down before the forces of reaction. In Mossley Division, the Cooperative and Labour forces worked splendidly together, but the Division was lost. Against 17,017 votes polled for the 'National' candidate, Mr Gibson polled 15,587 votes. The

Co-operative-Labour poll, however, had remained remarkably firm (Nally, 1939 p.12).

Over forty years on, Tess still retained trenchant opinions of the betrayal,

> It was disgusting. I thought it would never work (the National Government). I wasn't very old then but I remember it all perfectly well and this J H Thomas and Snowden and all that gang. They were for it of course, but it was all wrong and we were betrayed. But I didn't think Ramsay MacDonald would have gone in with them. But he wasn't a real socialist, he was all talk. He was a handsome man and a very good orator, but I don't think he really felt for the Labour Party as he should have. This J H Thomas, you see he resigned and he was the one who led the railwaymen to go back.

As the daughter and wife of miners, her real venom was kept for J H Thomas, whom she blamed for the collapse of the General Strike, which had left mining families struggling on alone for seven months. She, like many others from the mining community, never forgave him.

There was no option however, but to set about rebuilding the Labour and Co-operative Parties. It was a hectic period with many hours spent attending meetings in the evening with Tess of course deeply involved. She was active in the Women's Co-operative Guild and the Regional and Divisional Labour Parties. She became the only female member of the Board of Management of Denton Co-operative Society. She was in demand as a speaker for she was well informed with considerable wit. Tess laid great store in her appearance and was recognised as being well-dressed and stylish. This was a trait she passed onto her two daughters who always appeared in public meticulously dressed. She exemplified the old working class saying, 'It's no use being poor and looking poor!'

In 1935, the family moved to Blackley as Tom felt it would be easier for his political activities if they lived within the boundaries of the City of Manchester. Two years later in 1937, there was a by-election in the Openshaw Ward and Tom was elected unopposed to Manchester City Council.

With the benefit of several years' experience as a district and county councillor, Tom threw himself into his new role and quickly built up a high level of respect. His rise within the Labour Group was meteoric and within a few years was elected its leader. His full-time job also allowed him to develop networks thus facilitating even closer working relations between the Labour and Co-operative Parties in the Greater Manchester area. Furthermore, as Parliamentary constituency agent for Mossley he had to do the detailed preparatory work for the expected General Election of 1940 - the election that never happened because of the outbreak of the Second World War.

As the three younger members of the family were growing up in the 1930s, they found it surprisingly easy to adapt to the more urban area of Manchester. It proved to be an exciting and enjoyable time for them. The two girls were attractive teenagers and much of their social lives was centred on the Labour League of Youth. Both Alice and Win have written of what a gloriously, happy time it was for them.

Will, being five years older, not surprisingly was becoming increasingly involved in more formal political activities. For five years from 1930, he was President of the Manchester Labour League of Youth and from the following year sat on the national committee. He had left school and was working in local government as a solicitor's clerk whilst attending night school. Soon he was to move to work at the Co-operative Press in the city eventually switching over to become a journalist.

But dark clouds were looming over Europe which were to change all their lives. As both twins often said they were the generation who had their youth cut short by the Second World War. In a sense they were better prepared for it than Tess. They both had friends who had gone to Spain as members of the International Brigade to fight Franco and Fascism.

In their personal lives, mixing with the opposite sex moved onto marriage with Will marrying local girl, Hilda Clarkson, in 1937. Win was next, when on her 21st Birthday on 30 September 1940, she married Ronald Barber. She had been going with Ron for some years and even seen him off from Mosley Road Bus Station in Manchester when he had left to travel to Spain to fight the right wing Nationalists. The twins had planned to have a double wedding, but Alice's fiancée, Bill Lister, was overseas serving in the Royal Artillery so they had to wait a few more weeks for his leave when they also 'tied the knot'. Although Ron had a reserved occupation in skilled engineering work, in 1942 he joined the Royal Navy, serving as a chief petty officer on the aircraft carrier, HMS Implacable.

Will also joined the army to fight Hitler and served as a gunner in the 9th Field Regiment of the Royal Artillery until 1942 when he was medically discharged. But he felt it essential that the British people be kept fully aware of the happenings of the war and became an accredited war correspondent with the *Daily Herald* and then under the wartime pool arrangements for the *Reynolds News* and the *Observer*.

In 1945 Will was selected as the Labour and Co-operative candidate to fight Bilston in Staffordshire but on the edge of Wolverhampton which was a marginal Conservative Constituency. He gained the seat with a massive majority of almost 17,000, much to the delight and pleasure of all the Nally family. He was to hold it comfortably in the two following General Elections but his health was failing and he retired at the 1955 General Election at the age of 44.

Tess wasn't really surprised with this turn of events and later commented,

> He had a great fight but he wasn't well you know, he had cancer. He had one lung removed but it attacked the other one. I never really thought it would work when he got elected because I knew he hadn't the strength and they didn't have Saturday meetings. He used to come home Friday afternoon, in the house and have his bath and change. Then he would have to travel to Wolverhampton you see, to be there to do his surgery work. The men would have Sunday meetings.

All the pressure caught up with Will and in 1954 he announced he was not going to contest the seat at the following General Election. He didn't want to give up his Parliamentary work for he had built up a considerable reputation at Westminster. He hoped he might be adopted for a more northerly seat and in fact had a half promise from members in Manchester Gorton but although he was nominated for the seat when it came vacant for the 1955 General Election, he wasn't selected.

When the Second World War began in 1939, Tess's life altered dramatically. Like many Labour Party activists she initially had mixed views on the outbreak of war. She had seen the horrors and effects of the First

World War and how it had caused so much suffering to many working-class families. Equally, she was aware of the threat to her dreams and beliefs if the Nazis controlled Europe. In Manchester she had seen the strong-arm methods of Mosley's fascists and their hatred of the Labour Party. Furthermore, she knew some of the twins' male friends who had travelled to Spain to take up arms against Franco's army.

After the war was finally declared, there was a political truce between the main political parties. The routine work of these local parties was suspended and as a consequence many of Tess's activities disappeared. Initially she turned more of her attention to her family. Following the marriage of the twins she had the added worry about her two sons-in-law who, like Will, were in the forces fighting the Germans.

Tom, on the other hand, found himself even busier following the out-break of the war. As everyone on the home front pulled together, Tom's experience of local government coupled with his recognized administrative skills, found him in much demand to help tackle the problems facing a major industrial centre such as Manchester. He was co-opted onto numerous committees and ad hoc bodies running the city and wider afield. As Tess' skills became less in demand, Tom's workload increased.

As the air raids began over Manchester, Tom made use of his mining skills, obtained some pit props and used them to safely shore up the cellars of their home. Domestically, Tess' life changed as she became a grandmother once more, as Win gave birth to a baby daughter, Tessa, in August at Prestwich Maternity Home. Tessa was an addition to Will's two sons, Mike who was born in 1939 and Paul two years later.

She expected to be a grandmother again a little later when Alice became pregnant but tragically the baby was still-born. In her biography, Win described the awful experience when she had to carry a cardboard box containing the dead baby's body across Manchester on the bus. In those days maternity homes had no responsibility for the body following a still-birth. They just passed the responsibility onto the family. In Alice's case, the stillborn baby was simply handed to Win in a cardboard box to deal with. Tom was so disgusted by the practice that he called in the medical officer of health and the town clerk and initiated a campaign in Manchester to stop the despicable practice. At the personal level, eventually a happier situation prevailed, when Bill, Alice's husband, returned from the forces and they had a daughter, Marlaine, in 1948 and a son, Tom, in 1958 (Wheable-Archer, 2010 p.37).

All the demands of wartime, followed by the post-war rebuilding of the city and its communities, wreaked a heavy physical toll on Tom. He had pushed himself to the limit and his health began to fail. However, disregarding this, he worked incessantly as leader of the Labour Group and the Council, to rebuild the shattered, badly bombed City. He fought hard for the establishment of overspill estates outside the City boundaries such as at Mobberley in Cheshire and was vehemently opposed to high-rise development. Throughout the 1950s, he suffered from a series of heart attacks and then on 20 December 1956, had a massive one and died in the Jewish Hospital in the City at the age of 63.

Tess explained the background,

> But he had heart trouble you know, 'cos he really worked very, very hard. You see he would do a day's work, come home and have a bath, then he would ride out on his bike to the villages to the outside of Nottingham. He worked himself too hard. And the man at the Town Hall (Manchester) told me he would never wait for the lift and right to the top of the Town Hall he'd be going you know. He would never wait for the lift. He would forget he had a heart trouble and he had. That was through pit work of course. But he was in hospital before you see and then Will took over the work (the Co-operative Party secretary) for him for a short time but then of course he died.

Tom had always burnt the candle at both ends for even when he got home after meetings he turned to his books. Win recalls that their home was always full of books and Tess confirmed this, declaring that he just loved reading, especially history. He also appreciated good literature, notably Dickens and Hardy, but not surprisingly his favourite novelist was the leftwing Jack London. Then there were always the newspapers and he devoured the *Daily Herald* and the *Reynolds News* on a Sunday.

The work as Leader of Manchester City Council was awesome. It was one of the most important cities in the UK and Tom never shirked a challenge. He was council leader when local government in general and Manchester in particular was at the pinnacle of its power and influence.

Manchester City Council had responsibility from employing midwives to issuing death certificates and almost everything in between. It owned Thirlmere, a hundred miles to the north, as well as the developing airport of Ringway to the south. As leader he had a number of other important external roles including Deputy Chairman of the Manchester Ship Canal, National Chairman of the Housing and Town Planning Association, as well as serving as a Justice of the Peace. Furthermore, in the year of his death he was also Chairman of the demanding Council's Finance Committee.

Tom and Tess Nally at a Civic Reception in Manchester Town Hall
in the early 1950s

Regardless of all the previous health warnings, Tess was devastated by Tom's death. Her spirit was broken and although she was only sixty-one she began to withdraw from public life. Then, when her only son Will died of cancer in August 1965 aged 50, she found she couldn't carry on and her withdrawal was complete. Yet her mind remained active as did her interest in politics. She followed political matters very closely and right up to her death at the age of 93 on 10 April 1988, she still religious-ly tuned into Today in Parliament. The loss of the two men in her life, husband Tom and son Will, had a profound effect on her. Her two daughters, although both were deeply involved in public service, remained in close contact and looked after her.

Perhaps Alice best outlined the background to the Nally family's beliefs in socialist public service, 'We were born into the movement…Taken as small children to meetings of the Labour Party, where it was the custom to open with a socialist song, my sister and I were word perfect with the "Red Flag", "the International", "These things shall be" and "England Arise".' (Wheable-Archer, 2010 p.48).

In her early thirties as a young married mother, Alice was elected to the management committee of the local co-op, Failsworth Industrial Society, and became chairman of its Education Committee. She fully supported her husband Bill Lister as a Manchester City councillor, who served with distinction until his untimely death on 18 November 1975, aged 58. She herself had been appointed a magistrate, and continued for thirty years becoming the highly respected chair of the Juvenile Panel. In the 1970s she was elected to Manchester City Council for the Miles Platting Ward. In 1981 however, in order to be nearer to her daughter, she moved to Wigan and was elected to Shevington Parish Council; the village where her mother Tess was born.

The other twin Win, led an equally successful life of public service as a local government officer and later, elected councillor. In her first-rate autobiography, she provides a detailed account of her fascinating and active life. Win spent over thirty years in local government, retiring as a senior official in the City of Leeds in 1980. Her career had begun in her native Nottinghamshire, progressed in Salford and Manchester before finally ending in Leeds. She was highly respected and always at the forefront of progressive thinking, repeatedly bringing forward innovative ways to improve the lives of ordinary people.

One downside to this work as a senior local government officer was that she was restricted by convention in what she could do politically. She had joined the Labour Party at sixteen and remained a member all her life but it wasn't until she worked in Leeds and lived in the West Riding of Yorkshire in 1964 that she could again play her full part in Labour Party activities. She had moved to the village of Upper Denby near Huddersfield and it wasn't long before Win was making her presence felt in the local community. She stood unsuccessfully for the council in 1967 and again in 1970 when she was elected to sit on Denby Dale UDC until its abolition in 1974. She remained on the successor parish council becoming chair in 1981. In 1982 she was elected to the powerful Kirklees Metropolitan Borough Council becoming chair of its Social Services Committee until her retirement in 1987 when she left the council to help look after her elderly mother

She was prominent in revitalising the Denby Dale Branch of the Labour Party which became the dominating political force within the area. As she described,

> Political education was a feature of every meeting and social events included coffee mornings and evenings, pea and pie suppers, Halloween Parties, fashion shows, bonfire night parties and Easter Bonnet Parades, always supported by parents and children.

It was almost transferring the camaraderie of spirit of Nottingham and Manchester of the 1920s and 1930s into the modern age. The branch had a broad social cross section with all three Kirklees councillors being Labour; Colin Watson a miner, Bill Gregory a trade union official and Win. It was a high point for Labour in Denby Dale.

Win was always shocked and angered at the ignominy and injustice endured by ordinary people as witnessed when she described the experiences of particular rank and file party members, Harold and Nellie Auckland in the 1970s,

> He told how he was paid lower wages, by Kenyon's because he had a war pension for his disability. (Slight nervous impairment)... In their old age, they felt more financially secure with state pensions than ever they had been on piecework or short time at the mill (Wheable-Archer, 2010 p.104).

I too knew the couple and shared Win's affection for them. I find her comments a useful reminder of the injustice still prevailing and what ultimately underpinned the spirit and values of the Nally dynasty.

Alice, encapsulated so aptly the undying aspiration of the dynasty when in a speech to the South Lancashire Fabians in 1995, she declared, 'The party, born in 1900 should, in 1995 be more than a political party. It should be a faith and positive force for good, from security from fear, for justice at work, nurture for families. A crusade to deliver people from the tyranny of poverty, prejudice and the abuse of power. We have a great task ahead' (Wheable-Archer, 2010 p.51).

However, the final words on the Nallys, ought to go to the other twin, Win, who wrote of Tess and Tom, 'The life of neither can be contemplated separately. They were a partnership of complete integrity and complemented each other - Tom and Tess Nally. Together they had a full life with many joys and sorrows. They knew most of the leading lights in the Labour movement and were respected and admired' (Wheable-Archer, 2010 p.22).

Quotations of Tess Nally from interview with David Clark, 14 September 1978.

4

Willie Brook
1895-1979

James William Brook, or Willie as he was known, was born in Longwood on 5 December 1895. Longwood was a township on the western edge of Huddersfield immediately adjacent to the Colne Valley Constituency and indeed for Parliamentary purposes part of it fell within that constituency. His home at 103 Longwood Gate was on the edge of the Pennine Hills. It was in a row of terrace houses built of the local millstone grit and was typical of the homes of the textile workers in this part of Yorkshire. This was the land of chapels and mill chimneys but the vista to the front was across a valley to green fields leading onto the wild, desolate and windswept moors.

By the year he was born, politically the Labour movement in the locality was beginning to flex its muscles. It was one of the first areas in Britain where independent Labour Representation was being realised with Labour Parties or Unions, as they were initially called, having become firmly established in both Colne Valley and Huddersfield. They had successfully challenged the established Conservative and dominant Liberal Parties at the ballot box, having elected a county councillor as early as 1892 and followed this up with a number of local district councillors.

At the 1895 General Election the Independent Labour Party had contested both local seats. In Huddersfield, the candidate was H Russell Smart who polled 1594 votes or 11.2 per cent. Meanwhile, the Colne Valley activists had achieved a great coup by persuading the renowned trade union leader and the then general secretary of the ILP, Tom Mann to be their candidate, causing considerable excitement with his attracting 1245 votes or 13.4 per cent. In an area dominated by the wool textile industry, in which it was notoriously difficult for the unions to organise, this was a very creditable result. Willie's father would undoubtedly have heard Tom Mann speak either at the Longwood Labour Club, which had been founded as early as November 1892, or at one of his many open-air meetings.

Although radical politics were being widely discussed, religion still retained a firm hold in this part of Yorkshire with the non-conformist chapels continuing to attract many textile workers and their families. Even the newly formed Labour movement appreciated this and responded by establishing Socialist Sunday Schools (SSS) and Labour Churches where the ethical appeal of socialism was nurtured and widely emphasised. Politically, Tom Mann himself often spoke in religious terms and indeed in 1893 was even contemplating becoming a curate in the Church of England (Mann, 1923 p.92). Victor Grayson elected as Colne Valley's MP in 1907 had trained as a Unitarian Minister and frequently used biblical phrases (Clark, 1985 p.159). Later, the speeches of another local MP, Philip Snowden, were often referred to as in a 'come to Jesus style.' Willie's parents were regular chapel goers and naturally their large family went as well. Willie was one of twelve children although a number of his siblings died during childhood. In essence he was a member of a typical family of West Yorkshire textile workers.

His father Sam, was a radical and a member of his trade union. Longwood had somewhat of a tradition of trade unionism with Allen Gee, the general secretary of the principal union, the General Union of Textile Workers, living there. As early as 1892, Gee was elected to Huddersfield County Borough Council for the Lindley Ward as a Labour Union and Trades Council candidate and was also a member of both the Colne Valley and Huddersfield Labour Unions.

Initially Sam Brook had been a Liberal but in the 1890s was converted to socialism as a result of listening to the propagandists at the numerous outdoor meetings in Longwood. He attended the Labour Club which wasn't surprising as the secretary lived just across the road in the same street. Astutely, over seventy years later, Willie recalled that in truth, 'Really, what converted my father was through his stomach. He'd had to work hard and bring a family up'. This honest appraisal reflected the position of many working men of the period.

Willie had a happy childhood, growing up in the early years of the new century playing in the streets around his house and in the open country-side a little to the front. He attended the local board school as well going to the Sunday school in the Baptist Chapel. He admits to having been somewhat spoiled in that being the youngest of twelve and, with all the others working, they occasionally gave him presents. Furthermore, he was quite musical and learned to play the piano which was to serve him well over the years.

There wasn't a Socialist Sunday School (SSS) in Longwood but there was in Lockwood, Paddock as well as one in Huddersfield town centre which was to survive for many years. Willie however didn't attend the one in the town centre preferring to make the shorter journey to nearby Paddock.

> They were teaching socialist precepts. There were ten socialist commandments. I wish I could remember them, 'Love learning which is the food of the mind. Be as grateful to your teachers as to your parents. Do not think that he who loves his own country should hate and despise other nations or wish for war which is a remnant of barbarism'. There were socialist hymns. They weren't on Christ, same as 'England Arise'. There isn't much about Christ in 'England Arise'.

Willie recalls that socialist songs were regularly sung at Labour meetings right up to the Second World War as well as at the Socialist Sunday School. Often they used the standard hymn tunes but the words were by socialist writers such as Edward Carpenter. He refers on a number of occasions to the *Socialist Sunday School Tune Book* which was published in 1912. 'I wish I had kept them hymn books now because there were some lovely words in them. Now we had one,

> Forward! the day is breaking,
> Earth shall be dark no more;
> Millions of men are waking
> On every sea and shore. (SSS Hymn 74)

It's taken out of the *Baptist Hymn Book*. It's 'Onward the March is Onward', in theirs. And it's 'Stand up for Jesus', that tune.

He cites other favourites direct from church hymn books including the *Primitive Methodist*...;

> When wilt Thou save the people Lord
> O Lord of Mercy when?
> Not Kings and Lords but nations
> Not thrones and Crowns but men. (Hymn 279)

It is easy to see why these words by Ebenezer Elliott struck such a chord with the early Labour pioneers. The author recalls quoting it in the House of Lords, to be met with murmurs of approval from the Labour benches but stony silence from the Conservative and Liberals! (Lords *Hansard*, 31 March 2011, Col 1341).

One of the great favourites was written specifically for the Labour movement by the socialist Edward Carpenter,

> England Arise, the long, long night is over,
> Faint in the east behold the dawn appear;
> Out of your evil dream of toil and sorrow
> Arise, O England, for the day is here! (SSS Hymn 68)

Another hymn they often sang was;

> These things shall be! A loftier race
> Than e'er the world hath known shall rise
> With flame of freedom in their souls
> And light of science in their eyes.
>
> These things - they are no dreams - shall be
> For happier men when we are gone;
> Those golden days for them shall dawn,
> Transcending aught we gaze upon. (SSS Hymn 52)

It is not difficult to understand why these lyrics appealed so much to the early pioneers, reflecting as they do their political aspirations, ideals and dreams. The appeal of ethical socialism was centred on values and how to bring those ideals to practical fruition.

On 23 August 1976, Willie played these tunes on his piano in his home in Longwood and sang along with enthusiasm. Over the years they had-n't become dimmed in any respect. One of his favourites was sung to the American Civil War tune, 'Marching through Georgia'.

> The land the land,
> T'was God who gave the land.
> Why should we be beggars
> With the ballot in our hand,
> God gave the land to the people.

When he left school, Willie followed the family tradition and found work in the textile industry as a woollen piecener in a spinning mill. As time went by, he imbibed the radical politics of his father and joined the local Labour Union or Party. Meanwhile he continued to attend the Baptist Church and his political and religious beliefs intertwined in ethical socialism.

Longwood was one of the first areas in the district to have its own Labour club in autumn 1892 and it was to remain a staunch bastion of Labour support for the following quarter of a century. In the years around the turn of the new century, the movement came under considerable pressure and many of the Labour clubs failed. Longwood was one of only six in the Colne Valley Constituency to survive. The township had a resilient and determined group of Labour adherents who used the club as the base from which to espouse their cause. But the club provided more than just a venue for political activity. It became a social centre for its members. Lectures by visiting speakers on a wide range of topics were given and socials, dances and teas were held fortnightly and there was even a socialist choir for a period (Clark, 1981 p.109). In due course Willie became an active member of the club and it was there he developed his arguments and views and with them a life-long commitment to socialism.

In July 1907, Colne Valley was catapulted into the national political headlines when at a dramatic and exciting by-election it elected a charismatic young socialist, Victor Grayson, to be its MP. Grayson was only 25 years old with stunning good looks, a charming manner and brilliant oratory. Willie was only eleven at the time but was taken to one of Grayson's meetings by his mother where he met the flamboyant candidate whom he found to be, 'very pleasant and handsome and smartly dressed'. He came away impressed in particular by his speaking ability, recalling him as being, 'very forceful and always having a witty reply to hecklers. You should have seen the following he had to believe it. He really did stir things up. To me he seemed a torch-bearer, ready to set things on fire. He was a man with a message'.

The following year, the young schoolboy continued his political educa-tion when his parents took him to The Worker's Bazaar. *The Worker* was a very successful weekly newspaper published by the Huddersfield social-ists. In April 1908 in order to buy some new presses, it was decided to hold a bazaar in Huddersfield Town Hall to coincide with the annual conference of the Independent Labour Party which was being held in the town. It made a big impression on the young boy who could still describe it in detail over sixty years later. 'I'd never been in Huddersfield Town Hall. The stalls were wonderful. There was one an Indian palace, anoth-er Italian chateau, Holland a Dutch windmill and they were all linked together. Milnsbridge, Golcar and Longwood (the three most easterly townships in Colne Valley) shared one stall. There was so much stuff in the three day bazaar. Everything was decorated, Chinese cafe at the back of the platform'.

Willie's memory is extremely accurate and is confirmed in *The Worker*'s own report,

> ...facing the visitors as they enter the hall is the refreshment stall, which is designed as a typical English village, with a tiny church, surrounded by thatched cottages, pretty gardens, beehives, etc.. On the right is a Swiss Chalet, a castellated building representing Austria and Belgium, a colonial log hut, a gorgeous Indian palace and an Italian villa with its beautiful mosaic tile work. On the other side of the hall will be found a stall representing the land of Stars and Stripes. A wooden and plaster house typifying Norway and Sweden, a structure in the Russian style of architecture, a stone-fronted semi-castle house standing for Germany and a villa in 'gay Paree'. In the centre is a very picturesque Dutch windmill whilst another stall represents China. A Geisha tea-house and a Turkish divan smoke-room completes the list (*The Worker*, 25 April 1908).

It was clearly a most impressive event which illustrated the talent in the new political Labour movement. This tradition of holding annual bazaars and sales-of-work became part of the tradition of many local Labour parties for much of the twenieth century including in Colne Valley and Huddersfield. Willie enjoyed immensely formally opening the one in Huddersfield on the day before his eighty-first birthday, 4 December 1976, and took the opportunity to tell those attending the marvellous Worker Bazaar of 1908 which raised more than £1200 - an immense amount being equivalent to in excess of £100,000 in 2015 values.

By the time the First World War was declared in August 1914, Willie was eighteen and had already formed strong opinions against the conflict on both political and religious grounds. This was to be a seminal event of his life.

In the early years of the War, he was relatively unaffected for he simply refused to heed Kitchener's patriotic call and carried on working in the wool textile industry as normal. Of course he faced criticism and pressure from the patriotic majority of the population but he found support and succour in the Labour club where he discussed the issues of the day with other young men with similar views. As it happened, Willie wasn't as isolated in his opinions as might have been thought, for there were more conscientious objectors than usual in this part of Yorkshire. The Huddersfield area had one of the highest levels of individuals seeking exemption (Pearce, in ed. Evans, 2007 p. 23).

All this changed however in January 1916 when, as a result of a shortage of volunteers for the forces, the Military Service Act of 1916 introduced conscription which came into force on 2 March. Willie being eighteen, single and fit, was a prime candidate for military service.

He however had other plans. The Act had a clause which allowed those with strong conscience grounds against going to war to apply to the authorities for exemption from military service. It was a tortuous process through a series of tribunals and most of the applicants failed. Nationally, less than 17,000 gained exemption. There were individuals who did not appear before tribunals and if these are taken into account, Pearce estimates the total number of COs was between 20-23000 (Pearce, 2014 p.143).

Willie and a number of his friends were determined to resist conscription and were as yet unaware of the odds against them. He applied to the local tribunal in Huddersfield for complete exemption but this was refused. He was however, offered partial exemption as a member of the non-combatant corps of the army. These men were exempt from carrying guns but were otherwise full members of the army and undertook other tasks as the name implies. Willie never accepted the local tribunal's judgement.

Meanwhile the war was increasingly politicising him. He recalls going to a large meeting in Huddersfield which he describes so clearly,

> I was there that night, I was under arrest and I was there. If the bobbies would have known me they would ha' nabbed me. Victoria Hall and it was in February 1917. I hadn't long to go as I was nabbed. But I was keeping out of the way. I wanted to go as long as my uncle Ronnie because I knew at t'bottom, I wouldn't give in. Arthur Dawson was spotted that night and they arrested him. Course, they didn't know me as well. If the bobbies would have known me they would have nabbed me.

> He was speaking was Philip Snowden and they were hollering at the door was soldiers. They'd brought them in. They burst in and the door was by the platform. They got under the platform. Mrs Snowden got between one of them and they couldn't get at him right. They nearly got hold of him but they were jumped on. He was saved. Threw them off the platform, the meeting did. Snowden was against the war, so was MacDonald, he had to get through a window in the middle of one meeting somewhere in the Midlands. Well Philip never had nothing like that. But they came that night and said, 'Snowden, lets rip him'. They'd canes to slash him with. A soldier said he was going to slash Snowden's face with it. I saw that scene. The meeting was all powerful, they hadn't a chance, they threw them out.

> They said he married an aristocrat, Ethel Annakin. She was well brought up but she was a fine speaker. I'll never forget her that night. She stepped forward, somebody called out, 'Let's have a word from Mrs Snowden'. She stepped forward and gave a short speech and said, 'When that unruly mob burst into this room, they'd have me to tear to pieces before they'd have touched a hair

of the man I love'. She finished her speech, 'Workers of the world unite, you have all to gain and nothing to lose but your chains'.

For logistical and practical reasons, the army didn't want all the conscripts at once and introduced a phased recruitment. Eventually Willie received his call-up papers which he ignored and then failed to report for duty on 5 February 1917. He was then deemed to be 'on the run' although he continued living at home. The authorities didn't seem to move with great speed and it wasn't until 14 May 1917 that he was arrested as an absentee.

His experiences following the arrest had such an effect on him that almost sixty years later, he still had those memories as a conscientious objector etched deeply in his mind. He could recall them with clarity and describe them in graphic and moving terms. There is no better way to relay those experiences than in Willie's own words.

I was 21 years old when they arrested me, May 14 1917. They came to our house for me and I hadn't got up that morning, about 9 o'clock. Two men in the house and they were very nice and polite. I said, 'You'll wait until I get a snack of breakfast?' 'Oh yes,' they said, 'but don't be too long because we want to get in at this morning's court and it'll be better for you than stopping in the lock-ups in Huddersfield 'til Wednesday'. So I was just in time for the morning court on Monday morning. It was the 14th, I'll always remember it because it was Huddersfield Cattle Fair Day and I went on the train to Halifax after. I got to Halifax and I got leave that night to come home and I promised to return to Halifax by such a time on Tuesday morning and I was there.

I was taken to Ripon where the regiment was and of course when I got there I found some more COs in the guardroom. They'd refused orders. Some of them had been at Wormwood Scrubs and were waiting another sentence and I knew a few from Huddersfield. I was quite happy in the guardroom with them. I refused to put khaki on and my court martial came up and I was sentenced to two years with hard labour in Wormwood Scrubs.

We were taken down on the train about ten days after, 27th May it was, and it was just a week before Whitsuntide and a lovely spring day. We got out of the station and walked, they didn't show you up on the road if you walked ordinary - they didn't bother with you- and then we arrived at Wormwood Scrubs about 4 or 5 o'clock and went in. We'd to have a big bath straight off and to strip off. They put me in a cell which they said was temporary. The day after, I was taken before the governor and the laws of the prison were read out what I had to obey. You couldn't talk, you hadn't to speak to any- body only when you were spoken to, that was the rule.

I was put in a cell and as it was hard labour, I had to do without a mattress. Anyhow the canvas officer came round and he were a little bit sympathetic as he dared be. 'I'll give you a tip,' he says, 'you can make a bed of these canvasses you know'. I said, 'I'll do that'. I had a couple of bedcovers and that but it were a hard board to sleep on.

I were taken to the brush shop, to make brushes, hard brushes and hand brushes and I worked in there. There were a lot more came with me and we hadn't to talk, mind you we did get a word in when we could and I got caught there a bit. I had a punishment. I had a week in my cell, working in my cell for that. So I thought, well I mustn't get too much of this.

Wormwood Scrubs as a prison is four blocks. Four storeys high, forty-four each landing and forty-four cells on each side and there are four landings, one above another. You could go up an iron stair- case in the middle and we were on the top floor. My number, I'll always remember it, was 84. I was on that landing for my first twelve months and I was a brush maker.

They asked me what religion I was and really I would have liked to go to the Quakers but I didn't. It would have been better, you could say you were a Quaker and go to their meetings. I said I was a Baptist and I was put down for Baptist service. A very nice chap he was and he said if there were any of us that didn't see us rela- tives much, he'd write to them.

I took on with him. He was a nice old man. He belonged to the Baptist Tabernacle in Shepherds Bush and he wrote to our folk and told them how he found me because I told them they hadn't to come down to London - it was a long way for a bit of time they'd have with me and I never saw them.

Well you see the point was, when you'd been in six weeks, you were taken before a tribunal and I had a leaflet given and they offered me alternative work if I could prove myself genuine. I should have alternative work outside prison and it'd be better for me. I knew there were centres, one were at Dartmoor and the other was at Wakefield. It was accepted that I could be transferred there and it'd be much easier, would life that way. Of course I studied it out before I went and my sister said I should accept it. I shouldn't miss it and I wouldn't languish in prison. I said I wasn't going to say what I'm going to do yet. Anyway I made my mind up that I wasn't accepting it.

There was a row of us waiting to go into the tribunal and I think it was Lord Salisbury who was the chairman. He was very nice and said had I considered this leaflet. I said, 'Yes very much,' and he said was I going to accept it if I was proved genuine. I said, 'No I'm not going to accept it'. He says, 'Well I'm surprised at you. You know you've a two year sentence here and it's not a nice place for you to be in. If I were you I'd have a little bit more time to think it over'. I said, 'Thank you very much but I don't think it'll change my mind'. So I came out and I don't know if there were any more in the group accepting or not.

That morning I went on with my sentence. When I got to the brush shop I found that they weren't accepting it neither, you see. I'd get a word in with them when I could but you couldn't get much conversation.

I did my sentence in the brush shop, the first twelve months sentence but that were really ten months if your behaviour was good, but I'd lost a day's remission because I was caught talking. Meanwhile while we were in there, they'd worked for some concessions for us outside, to have more exercise and be able to talk a little bit. Well this was the concession they gave to me when we'd be in a twelve months sentence. I was moved into another part of the prison and put on canvas work and you could exercise twice a day. I think it was half an hour and you could walk round in twos and threes, conversing. But you know it was a bit boring. You can't always find something to talk about when one hadn't had a letter or anything like that. The only news we got in prison was at the service on a Sunday afternoon and they'd give the weekly news out. They'd tell us what they wanted us to know, that's all. When you went to chapel, you know, there was no looking at your next neighbour. If you did, the warders spotted you and you had to go to the front. You see they were so tight. You could sing as well as you wanted but you hadn't to speak and look only in front of you and there were a good many of us who were at the back of the church.

The other convicts were in the front half and you could distinguish us because we had different uniforms; ours was a grey suit marked with white arrows and theirs was a fawn suit marked with black arrows. When the service was over they marched us back to our cells. That was on a Sunday, then there was a service again on the Wednesday morning at the church for half an hour and that was all there was, except for when the Baptist service was on. I went to that, half an hour. That's the only entertainment there was in that place. There were no concerts, nothing at all.

And the diet, well a pint of porridge, a cup of cocoa, I think it was, and a slice of bread. The dinner was brought round. The best was on a Thursday to me, a bit of gravy on the meat and that. I just forget, one dinner was potatoes and some kippers, small ones and peas. They weren't appetising but you'd to learn to eat them. The porridge, you'd to get that down in the morning and then supper at 4 o'clock and nothing else and you'd to save some of that bread until the morning after. I just forget what else there was but it was very plain. It was just keeping you alive. You were weighed every week, they were watching your weight and they were just keeping you alive. There was no change at all. The best day was Thursday, you got pea soup in summertime and a kind of gravy and meat in winter.

You had to be in bed at 8 o'clock and you were awakened, I couldn't just swear to the hours now, but it was round half-past-seven or something like that and then you had to tidy up your cell. You had to keep your cell clean and tidy. Every morning they would walk round and anything out of place was reported. What you had to wash in was a disgrace, a little tin bowl not much bigger than those pudding things and then you were taken to the bath house once a week for a good wash and clean clothes put on. You hadn't your own clothes. You had your own trousers and coat and that but underpants and that, somebody else could have worn them before. They were all washed in the laundry.

We had to be in bed at 8 o'clock and they'd come round at 8 o'clock and if you weren't in bed, 'What are you doing out of bed, get into bed at once'. The cell windows were as high as that door top here and you'd get a buffet and stand on the look-out and if you were caught you could be reported for looking out of the window.

They brought your breakfast. About 7.30 or quarter to eight, it was brought round. You'd a pot in your cell and a dish to put it in and you'd to keep that clean too. They brought a tin with the food on, not much variety. I had to shovel that down all at once for the day. We just kept body and soul together.

After breakfast you had to get ready for the exercise and I forget how long. I think it was half an hour or something like that. Then if you were on associated labour, go down to the workshop and work in the brush factory. The brush maker, Mr Heath, was very nice. He spoke to you very nice but that was when nobody else was about. I liked him very well, mind you he had to teach us and look after us. Roberts, the warder who stood at the door, he was watching that we didn't talk. That's him that reported me and he said to me once after, '84 you be careful, you know you've had one dose'.

I had a two year sentence and I went in May. Well of course, I have to admit the first three months were a bit of tension when I was on my own. Bit of fretting you know but I had to try and shake it off and it went on. I was hoping the war would end before I got out but it didn't and I made my mind up that I couldn't go on in here for two years having to do this, no good worrying.

The letters, the first letter came when I had been in eight weeks. They could inquire every day how I was going on but I couldn't inquire about home. They wrote many a time to see how I was.

The first No-Conscription Fellowship was organised in Huddersfield and it was a good NCF, very strong. I knew nothing about it until January 1917 when someone told me and I went down. I was that interested. I found out that a lot of young socialists were in, such as Arthur Dawson and Arthur Gardiner. All of them were in and of course there was a community from the

Quakers came too, Well you see, you got a little bit of courage. My sister joined so she could get to know.

You could have seven books sent in if you wanted after such a time but I didn't bother. There were religious books and educational books and there were books of fiction. The librarian came round every week to know what you wanted. Oh yes I was able to read that way, that did help me. It passed the time. I got interested in it too, I had to. It helped to wear the monotony down and I was looking forward to getting back to my social time to get on with my reading. You went back to your cell on a Saturday dinnertime, slammed the door to and you knew then you were shut up all weekend unless you went to church on the Sunday.

We had exercises every day, every morning but as I say when we'd had a twelve month sentence, we'd two exercises a day. They got that granted for us. Yes, we were always parading around - I can see the ring yet.

The lavatories were on the landing. You had to ring a bell in the hours but if you wanted it at night, you had to use it in your cell and then clear out the morning after.

I was put to it after Wormwood Scrubs. It came did the release in January. I was in Wormwood Scrubs when the Armistice was declared. Just after I got on that special, I had to work in the canvas shop and my word there was a strict warder. He didn't warn you. He caught you once, he reported you. I thought, he's not catching me, I've had enough. You see I was used to it. I could do without it and the poor beggars when they were coming they wanted to start talking and they were caught. Anyway as it came close to the end there were some old bits of cloth came in from Yorkshire, suiting and stuff. Mr Sawyer, the head warder he got to know us, he said, 'You've worked in the mill haven't you?' I said, 'Yes I have'. He said, 'Do you know anything about this?' and I said, 'It's a bit of wool isn't it, woollen goods?' He says, 'Well they wanted them all turning up, separating the linings and that'. He says, 'I'm going to put you in charge, to take it round for them and look after it and then bag it up'. He didn't say will you do it. He says, 'You'll be able to do it', and I said, 'Well I should hope so'. I thought it'd be a bit of exercise and you see I could go to each man then and speak to them.

Of course there were some who said how long have you been in here and I don't know how you've stuck it. It's cruel isn't it? I said you mustn't think that. Think of the time when you get out and it'll come. I got hardened. I had to harden myself up, and not bother. It went on 'til that day and my release came on the 21st January.

I was in when the Armistice was declared, we knew that. The hooters went up at 11 o'clock and in that shed, they all sent up a cheer. They all cheered to death, to their hearts content. The warders never said nothing. Then we were taken to church in the afternoon and they read it out, the Armistice terms and that. Then of course, that was in November, 'cos I didn't want Christmas in. I'd had one birthday in and I was to have another in. I had my 22nd in and my 23rd and as Christmas came, no change of diet, just t'same.

In January 1919 my release came but I knew it wasn't a release. You see they hadn't given an armistice for us. I was taken down and given my clothes and the warder says, 'There's a lady waiting to see you. I don't know how she'll go on because there will be an escort there too'. I said, 'Well I'll have to settle that up'. So she came to see me and said, 'Are you Mr Brook?' She was a Quaker lady, Miss Ashby, and she said, 'I've been talking to your escort and he says "I was going to take you first and find you a meal but he's a London lad and he's wanting to go home to his wife and child and he's going to take you with him. So I mustn't say more now but is there anything you're short of, literature or books?" ' I accepted one or two things but I was well equipped and she stayed with me a good bit and then left.

They called this lad Alf Condon. He said, 'How long have you been in there?' and when I told him he said, 'Good God'. He said, 'How have you existed?' I said, 'Well I'm still here'. He says, 'Well I'm going to take you to my home for the day and then we shall catch the 4 o'clock to Lincoln. Your regiment is at Lincoln'. I said, 'What'll your wife say taking me'. 'Oh she'll not mind that', he says, 'She's having me for the day. She'll make you at home lad, you needn't worry. You'll have a happy day with us'. So he took me to his home and she said, would I have a kipper for breakfast? Well I said, 'I can eat anything'. So I had a kipper and there was another woman came in and he said, 'I've just fetched him out of Wormwood Scrubs. He's been in two year'. 'Good heavens, how have you lived in there?' He had a piano and he asked me if I could play. 'Well,' I said, 'I used to do a bit', and I played for him. We had a right good day there and a little child, she was about two year old, she was fair interested.

Of course we had to leave at such a time to get a train to Lincoln. We landed at Lincoln going towards the evening and I will always remember walking through the main street and seeing that archway. We walked under it and up the hill to the barracks. I was put in a room in the barracks. You see I had done nothing wrong then. I was treated ordinary. I had some supper brought.

Morning after, I was taken and ordered to put khaki on again and I refused of course. There was the same procedure. I said, 'Some of my relatives wish to see me. Will they be able to see me?' 'Oh yes they'll be able to see you son'.

They came did my mother and sister and nephew. They had come on Monday and went to see the ILP here and they found some lodgings for them. Of course there were plenty of ILPers there who were against the war and this Arthur Hayward and his wife took them in. They came up to see me and he said, 'We're looking after your mother and sister and nephew all right. They're quite happy with us Willie. You mustn't worry over them. They're in good company'.

He came a few times and then on the Saturday they were going back home, I said, 'Well I've been court martialled but I don't think there will be anything this weekend'. Directly they'd gone, they fetched me out again, led me out in front of the regiment; two years hard labour and I was going to gaol that afternoon. It was Albert who applied to take me. When he got me outside he says, 'Isn't your mother here?' I said yes and he said, 'Do you know where they are?' I said, 'Well I know the address'. We found them. When they saw me, they were surprised and I told them I was on my way to gaol. He said, 'But he isn't going straight in. He wants to stop with you for an hour or two. I can risk it'.

Well he filled the house and fetched some friends in. They had me on the piano playing and we had a right beano. Albert said he didn't want to get me into bother. 'You mustn't stop here too long lad. We don't want anybody else in bother'. A few of them went with us a little bit of the way. My mother and sister came home that day.

It was Saturday afternoon at the end of January 1919, when I knocked at Lincoln Prison door and I was taken in again for two years. Course I knew it would be commuted as well. I knew it were on the way. I had two years in Lincoln, mind you. It wasn't as good as Wormwood Scrubs. You see, Wormwood Scrubs there were more in and in Lincoln there were only five in.

I was put in my cell and they said Fenner Brockway was in. (Brockway was a prominent member of the ILP. Before his imprisonment he had been editor of its newspaper, *The Labour Leader* and had set up the No-Conscription Fellowship in November 1914). Had I anything for him Alf asked? And I said yes. I said, 'His wife's written to me' and we got a message to him and I told them what it was. It got to him some way. Then came a reply in the yard and I spotted him one day down in the baths.

I'd been in Lincoln a fortnight when the chief warder came to me and he said, you know they dare say a little bit more, he says, 'I'm sorry for such as you, you don't belong here. They didn't ought to keep you in here. You must do as you're told.' I said, 'I won't make it harder for myself'.

I had to work on associated labour with other prisoners and it went on. The principal warder came to me one afternoon and he says, 'Hadn't you a letter yesterday?' I says, 'I had'. 'Well,' he says, 'All were going on at home' Cos he'd read it you see - he had to do. He says, 'I've some bad news for you. Your father, he's passed away'. I says, 'Ooh, that's a bit of a shock, but he wasn't well'. 'You can get out for that', he says.

So I studied it over and I thought, I'll try it on. I'll see what writing to the Home Secretary about coming to the funeral. I put a petition in to see the governor and told the governor and he said yes. He says, 'I'm very sorry that something like this has happened to you'. He were a military man but he were a gentleman, I will say that. He were a decent fellow. He says, 'I'll see what can be done'. The chief warder says, 'Well, I've been pumping him if you can get to the funeral'. 'Well,' I said, 'they haven't said so yet but the funeral was on Saturday'. They came on the Friday morning that the Home Secretary had granted me temporary release and said, 'You'll have to give your word that you'll come back'. Which I did.

I was released on the Friday afternoon and I went straight to Cecil Street to them friends to tell them and he showed me to the station. I knew I had to change at Penistone and have a long wait. I found a barber's shop, 'cos I wanted shaving. I got home about nine and walked in on Friday night. My eldest brother had flu, he was married but he couldn't go to the funeral. He'd had that bad flu and it had laid him up. My elder sister said, 'Well it's a good job you've come because there will only be you and me and my mother of our own that can go'. We had a brother at the front somewhere but he hadn't heard then. The funeral was Saturday afternoon and they pleaded for them to give me while Sunday morning. They said he can't get back in time, and I had to return on the 8 o'clock train from Huddersfield on Sunday morning and go straight back.

When I got to Lincoln Station there were about thirty waiting for me, ILPers. They said, 'you aren't going back to gaol without going to the ILP rooms to have a drink'. I went and there was a fellow come to speak and I was introduced to him. When I got to Lincoln Gaol, there was Fenner Brockway there. I got messages to him.

But this was the interesting point in Lincoln Gaol. It was before I was released, one Monday night, there was such a stampede. The warders were running about and shouting. I thought what's up. Is the place on fire? Eeh, there was a kerfuffle. I got to know the morning after. When it was quiet, Alf told me, 'De Valera escaped last night. He got out of the back door and there was a motor car waiting and ran him straight to the coast'.

Before my release came I had a bad knee. I had squeezed a pimple and it had turned septic and I couldn't walk. Instead of walking out I had to walk into the hospital. It delayed me four days and I came out. It was the end of April when I came home. I was a wreck you know. After, the reaction set in and then the NCF, there had been a fund raised for us, for absolutists, to get us some help. That lad from Golcar, Herbert Hirst, he'd got home and he was waiting for me. We went on the second Monday in May and we set off for Scalby (Scarborough) and we'd go to Doves Court. They were taking them in for a week there. I met folk there and played the piano and my mate was the singer. There were some COs there that week and they were having a concert on the Monday night because some of them were going back two days after and of course we took part in it. We had a right happy week there and there was a woman and her husband from Dewsbury. They were Adult School people and they got right friendly with us. They said, 'You want to join the Adult Schools Movement, Willie, you'll find people broadminded there'. We did, we joined the Adult Schools and I've been an Adult Schools man ever since. Mind you I was a member of Salendine Nook Baptists and I was in the choir there. It's the anniversary on Sunday and we shall go. They were very nice with me there, I had no bother with them. I had things said to me.

We went to Scarborough, we could only stay in the guest house for a week and then we had to go to Wrea Head. They were a big Quaker family. We had the remaining fortnight at Wrea Head. It's a big estate between Scalby and Coulton on the hillside. It's the first time I've seen cows milked by electricity. The countryside was covered with daffodils and primroses. We had three glorious weeks. We did some walking about, rambling and that. After three weeks I came home and I was better built-up.

Of course my mother didn't want me to go and start working straight away. I says, 'Well I'm going to get some work'. I got in down at C & J Hirsts. The trade unions got me in and I got on all right. It's been said to me many a time things that weren't nice but I took no notice of them - they came round. I did very well. I worked at C & J Hirsts 21 years and then I went to Whitefords. I did 35 at Whitefords.

My brother that was in the forces, well, he didn't want to go but he was married. He went. He got to Italy. He came home at the same time. He didn't show it [any resentment] because he didn't want to go. He did all sorts of things to get out of going. So he couldn't say nothing but he didn't show any resentment. At my father's funeral his wife was there and aye, she was grand. She took me down to see her father and one of the kids that had been born. She showed no resentment did Edith. I was telling the youngest not so long ago what had happened to me. 'I never knew Uncle Willie that you went to prison'. I said, 'Have they never told you?' He said, 'No they've never said nowt'. I said, 'Well you have the history now. I was in gaol for two years'. There isn't so many in Longwood knows now, they're dead. Mind there are some.

Edie's [later to be his wife] father and mother were dead against the war and I was always in their favour. No. I've not had much bother and the Chapel, the Superintendent gave me a welcome back to Sunday School.

Following his return to Longwood from prison and after a period of rehabilitation, Willie gradually picked up the threads of his life including his political activities. He was to remain a Labour activist for the rest of his life.

At the General Election of 1918, he was not allowed to vote although he was pleased with the result in Colne Valley where Wilfrid Whiteley, who was anti-war, polled 9473 votes. Although he failed to win the seat it was a creditable performance and provided some indication of the attitude of the Labour voters in the constituency towards the war.

At the following election of 1922, he was delighted that both the Labour candidates for the local seats had been active in the anti-war campaigns. Jimmy Hudson in Huddersfield had been a conscientious objector and like Willie had been an absolutist serving a prison sentence in Wormwood Scrubs and elsewhere. He failed to win the seat by a narrow margin but went on to do so in the 1923 General Election.

However in Colne Valley, Philip Snowden was the Labour standard bearer and gained the seat which he held with increasing majorities until 1931 when he took a peerage and went with Ramsay MacDonald on his defection from Labour, joining the National Government as Lord Privy Seal. He soon became disenchanted with the National Government and resigned the following year.

Philip Snowden was somewhat of a favourite in Colne Valley. He had come to help Victor Grayson in the 1907 by-election and Willie recalled that he

came to Longwood every year when I was a child and he came right up to being an MP. When he became MP, there were crowds, morning, afternoon and night. He was a solid socialist. He wasn't frightened of being unpopular. If he said a thing it didn't matter what they said, he'd say what he hoped was right.

They adopted him as candidate for Colne Valley and they knew then that he'd gain it because he carried a lot of the radical vote. He wasn't liked by the extreme socialists. They tolerated him because he was carrying the day for 'em. He were a socialist all right. He carried a lot of the temperance vote. All the Liberals I knew went for him when he was temperance you see.

In 1931 when he left Labour and went with Macdonald to form the National Government, there was deep disappointment amongst the Labour supporters in Colne Valley. He didn't stand again but advised voters to support the Liberal candidate, Lance Mallalieu who won the seat.

He however lost in 1935 and later switched to Labour, winning a by-election in Brigg in 1948, a constituency he held until his retirement in February 1974. He came from a radical, local political family with his father Frederick, having been MP for Colne Valley, 1916-22, whilst his brother JPW Mallalieu (Bill), was a highly respected Labour MP for Huddersfield, 1945-79. In 1991, Bill's daughter Ann continued the political tradition when she became a Labour Life Peer.

Willie was saddened with Snowden and summed up the position thus;

> To me he was very bitter at the end but I think he was disappointed because he thought it was the best thing to do at the time. He told them he was a socialist as well as ever but they were bound to have to give way for the time being to save their financial problems. Mind ya, I didn't like what he did with us post office savings. They said ya know, us post office savings were in danger. They frightened folk with that.

But this bitter disappointment did not deflect Willie from following his deeply-held socialist convictions. Like most working-class people he was used to disappointments. Life was never easy and when faced with set-backs, they simply carried on. That was their way of life. Throughout his working life he understood the value of trade unionism and played a full part in his union. Furthermore he maintained always the importance of politics for ordinary people and remained active in the Labour Party until his death on 25 August 1979

In particular, he never forgot those experiences in prison as a CO which remained forever etched in his consciousness but not for a moment did he ever regret the stance he had taken. He was one of those few COs who were 'absolutists' as they were not prepared to accept any concessions. The numbers who took this position are unclear. Of the 4522 recommended to the Bryce Committee only 293 refused any compromise. The No-Conscription Fellowship estimated the figure in 1919 to be 1369 whilst Cyril Pearce's more recent research suggests a figure approaching 1400 (Pearce, 2014 p.155). Whatever the precise number, Willie Brook was one of those brave few who brooked no compromise whatsoever.

Willie Brook on left when he opened a Labour sale of work in 1976
(with JPW Mallalieu MP)

Quotations of Willie Brook from interviews with David Clark, 23 August 1976 and 12 September 1978.

5

Gladstone Mathers
1893-1984

Skelmanthorpe is a village in West Yorkshire, set amongst low rolling hills where the textile district meets the coalfield. Traditionally it was very much a working class community with the predominant employment being in the wool textile industry. Its population was relatively static and in 1911 was 3817. In recent years the improvement in the road network has seen the village become more attractive to commuters with the population increasing marginally to 4178 by the time of the 2001 Census. It was served by a railway station but the line was closed in 1983 to be replaced ten years later by the Kirklees Light Railway.

Although the majority of the employment was in the textile industry there was considerable amount of work in the various coal mines. Two pits dominated the local scene until the final quarter of the twentieth century, Park Mill near Clayton West and the Emley Moor Mine. In the latter case, the miners entered the mine by a deep shaft sunk from Emley Moor but the coal was brought out near the station in Skelmanthorpe from where it was transported to its markets. The coal spoil heaps were on the edge of the village and Gladstone Mathers estimated that perhaps up to a fifth of the men locally worked in these mines and the one or two other smaller ones. In fact, both Gladstone's elder brothers, Haydn and Harold began their working lives in the local pit as trammers before moving into the textile industry.

Until 1938, it had its own urban district council but in that year it was merged to form the Denby Dale UDC. Then in 1974, it became part of Kirklees Metropolitan Borough Council. For most of the nineteenth century it had been in the West Riding South Parliamentary Seat but in the re-organisation of 1885, it joined the newly formed Holmfirth Division where it remained until that seat was abolished in 1918. It then became integrated into Penistone until 1955 when it was transferred to Colne Valley. It remained there until 1983 when it moved to Dewsbury, then briefly into Wakefield before reverting again to Dewsbury.

Its politics have traditionally been of a radical nature. Initially it was represented by progressive Liberal MPs before switching allegiance to Labour in the early 1920s. Whilst the village was in the Holmfirth Division, its representative from 1885 until he resigned in 1912 was H J Wilson who was regarded as a radical Liberal MP, as was his successor in the 1912 by-election Sydney Arnold. In 1910 and 1912, Labour contested the seat but came third on each occasion. Arnold again became the MP on the formation of the new constituency of Penistone in 1918 but he resigned in early 1921 when the Yorkshire Miners put up one of their local activists William Gillis who captured the seat for Labour. However, at the General Election the following year he lost to the Liberals.

In these early years, the miners in Yorkshire were not as radical in their politics as they were to become later. There were a number of constituencies in Yorkshire which were dominated by miners and in some of these the Liberal Party reached an accommodation with the miners' leaders, and arranged for them to be elected as MPs under the Lib-Lab banner. As early as 1885, the President of the Yorkshire Miners' Association (YMA), Ben Pickard had been successfully elected as a Lib-Lab MP for Normanton which adjoined the northern edge of the Holmfirth Constituency. Pickard dominated mining politics in Yorkshire for twenty years until his death in 1904. He was a strong Liberal and in particular was bitterly opposed to the Independent Labour Party. This came to a head in a Parliamentary by-election in October 1897 when the ILP ran the trade union leader, Pete Curran, as candidate but Pickard threw the support of the YMA behind the successful Liberal candidate Joseph Walton, a coal owner from Durham.

Although Pickard was succeeded by two further Lib-Lab MPs, the tide was beginning to turn. In 1906, the YMA placed one of their members, J Wadsworth, into the Hallamshire constituency immediately to the south of Holmfirth as a Lib-Lab. By then, many of the younger miners were beginning to tire of the Liberals and turn to the ILP. Amongst these was Willie Lunn, who unsuccessfully fought the by-election in Holmfirth for

Labour in 1912, doubling Labour's share of the vote. In 1906, Herbert Smith a member of the ILP was elected President of the YMA and in the same year, the miners in Yorkshire voted to affiliate to the Labour Party. Two years later in a further ballot they confirmed that decision and the YMA became part of the Labour Party with its two sitting Lib-Lab MPs switching to Labour. The mood had changed. Over the following few years the miners switched their allegiance firmly to Labour with an increasing number of miners in Skelmanthorpe becoming active in the ILP and after the 1918 re-organisation, the Labour Party.

By the 1924 General Election, Labour had chosen a Workers' Educational Association lecturer, Rennie Smith as its candidate, and he regained the seat which he held until the 1931 General Election landslide. At the following election of 1935, Labour once again won the seat with a dentist H G McGhee and the party has retained it ever since.

Towards the end of the nineteenth century a number of individuals locally, as elsewhere, were beginning to tire of the charade of being represented by radical Liberals and were considering electing working men who would be independent of the two established parties. Some of the local textile workers in particular were in favour of independent representation of Labour and were aware that like-minded individuals in the neighbouring constituencies of Colne Valley and Holmfirth had actually formed local Labour Parties as early as 1891 in Honley and by 1905 in New Mill. Indeed some of the keener men in Skelmanthorpe began travelling to meetings in those villages.

Initially, the pioneers had attempted to achieve their objectives through a Mutual Improvement Society and following its failure, a Ratepayers Association. By 1906, it became apparent that these organisations were failing to meet their needs and desires. Thus in early July 1906, on the village's busiest day of Feast Sunday, they invited an ILP propagandist, Tom Myers, to visit the village and he spoke at an open-air meeting on the 'Gospel of Socialism'. The meeting was a success and encouraged the organisers with the result that Victor Grayson came to the village on 31 July 1906. Grayson was a fine orator and was to be elected MP for Colne Valley in a by-election the following year. Later in August another itinerant ILP propagandist, E Black addressed an open-air meeting on the topic of 'Workman's Hell and the Way Out'.

A few weeks later on 18 September 1906, the Parliamentary Labour

Candidate for Huddersfield at the General Election of that year, T Russell Williams, spoke in the village and at the close of the meeting it was decided to form a Skelmanthorpe branch of the Independent Labour Party with thirty-four members signing up very quickly.

Skelmanthorpe Labour Party in 1927
with David Mathers seated second from right in the second row

The branch had its 'ups and downs' but eventually became a force to be reckoned with. On 15 October 1927, it was sufficiently confident to organise a Coming-of-Age Celebration and a short history of the branch was compiled which fortunately has survived. A vivid account of the early pioneers emerges. Immediately followings its formation, the branch acquired a wooden hut which had been a barber's shop opposite the Commercial Inn on the main street which led to the Labour members being nicknamed 'the Little Wooden Hut Lot'.

Propaganda meetings continued and the party became well established on the local political scene. Towards the end of 1907 the party managed to raise six pounds to purchase other premises in Queens Street which formerly had been James Tickles' cobbler's shop.

In spite of their enthusiasm those early days were not always easy and the members faced opposition, hostility and ridicule. Being comprised almost entirely of working men and women, finance was a perennial problem and one means of raising cash was by holding public suppers.

In the brief history, an incident involving the gift of a suckling pig is recalled, which caused great amusement in the locality.

> To understand the joke it must be understood that when the pig was cooked it was so rich that the stomachs of the members couldn't stand it. During a discussion of the party in one of the public houses, one particular person said he was the only man who had ever stopped the mouth of the Labour Party. When some of the people had recovered from their astonishment, he was asked how he had done it. His reply was, 'Why I gave them a suckling pig'.

Then on 11 October 1911 the local activists received a great fillip. In the words of their leaders, it was, 'a red letter day in our history. The Grand Old Man of the Socialist Movement and the father of the ILP paid us a visit'. This was their hero, the Labour leader, Keir Hardie MP. They described the itinerary in detail. 'He was met at the station by the village brass band and they led a procession around the village to the meeting place at Pilling Lane Primitive Methodist Schoolroom'. The room was packed as, 'Many came out of curiosity to see a raving wild man, but found a mild-mannered peaceful person fired with the zeal of his message to the working classes of this country'.

This visit had a massive impact on the way in which the new party was viewed in the community. It made a lasting impression and sixty years later, many elderly Skelmanthorpe residents would recall the occasion. Gladstone Mathers remembered it and another fellow member George Stephenson gave the author a *Primitive Methodist Hymn Book* in which was pasted a photograph of Keir Hardie and reference to his meeting in the Schoolroom.

The following year, the pioneers established a boot and shoe business which they ran successfully for several years. During World War I, Labour members held divided opinions but many of the ILP activists were opposed to the War. In Skelmanthorpe, there were a number of conscientious objectors, most of whom were members of the ILP. Although this created some tension in the village, it caused no lasting effect on the emergence of the local Labour Party. In the 1927 'Coming of Age Report', it is recorded that,

The ILP policy during the war attracted several new members at its close, and the branch made headway until 1922, when we felt sufficiently courageous to purchase the property on which the club now stands. Again this was done on borrowed money (Coming of Age Report).

From those early days of struggle the Labour Party in the village went from strength to strength. The Skelmanthorpe Urban District Council was abolished in 1938 and was merged to form the Denby Dale Council. Following the Second World War, Labour normally dominated the council and when it in turn was abolished in 1974, there were 16 Labour councillors and 4 anti-Labour. The three councillors elected to the new body, Kirklees Metropolitan Council, were all Labour. Although since then the party's fortunes have fluctuated somewhat.

In the 1970s, the Skelmanthorpe local party was one of the largest branches in the Colne Valley Constituency with over sixty members and was very active. It met in its own headquarters building in the centre of the village. However the maintenance costs became prohibitive and eventually it was sold to Skelmanthorpe Brass Band in 1978.

This was the village where Gladstone Mathers was born on 20 March 1893 at 4 Garrett Buildings. Garrett Buildings had originally been a warehouse but had been converted into houses. He lived there with his father and mother and three brothers and two sisters. Gladstone was the third youngest in the family.

His father David was a handloom weaver and thus worked from home, principally weaving fancy vests and waistcoats. The arrangement was that Shepley Textile Company had a warehouse in the neighbouring village of Shepley and it was responsible for taking the orders which were then contracted out to the handloom weavers. David Mathers would walk the three miles to Shepley to collect the warps and wefts and to return the finished products. There were a number of handloom weavers in the village involved in this trade.

Their living conditions were poor as Gladstone himself described,

When I was born there were two looms in the room I was born in. In fact you can't imagine the conditions we lived in those days. It was typical of a lot of houses in Skelmanthorpe at that particular time. There were two looms and three beds in that same house. Screened off, you know, a whole wide-open bedroom and my parents had a bed, these shut-up beds in the corner of the house. Then when they got out of bed in the morning it shut up and looked like a chest of drawers. There was the living room and the bedroom in our house and there were six of us.

They all slept in the same room along with two handlooms each being over 36 inches wide.

When my father was in full work he would start handloom weaving according to the time of year. He'd get up earlier when there was more light but sometimes in order to save light he'd wait a little longer. We'll say anywhere from around half past seven if there was plenty of work until half past six or seven.

Gladstone slept on a mattress underneath the back of the handloom. He later recalled,

I've a picture now of the bed where I laid with my brother Sydney. It wasn't a bed, simply a mattress on the floor, that was all and often times he'd start working before we had to get up and often times in a spirit of mischievous sort of way we'd just keep getting hold of his treadle…and he'd remonstrate with us and tell us to give up but of course he was very considerate was my father. He didn't hide us so soon and then if we persisted in doing it I can see him now getting out of his loom and threaten to hit us with a rod. It was a hard life. As lads we didn't really understand. As my father said, we'd always some bread.

Gladstone started school at five and left in 1905 when he passed his leaving examination at twelve. This was a period when increasingly the use of handlooms was diminishing except for certain specialities but he did find work as a part-time wirer on a handloom, weaving plush in an individual's home and when he was thirteen he became full-time. The following year he moved to work for a short time in a local textile mill.

Then as he was approaching his fifteenth birthday, he returned to work alongside his father in his own home as a handloom pattern weaver. He carried on doing this for a little over a year when he moved with his father to work at Benjamin Armitage and Sons at the Shepley Warehouse and then in turn he also began working on power looms. Many years later in 1974 he recalled, 'I am the only person living in Skelmanthorpe now who can say that they were a weaver on a handloom in their own bedroom'.

His father took a deep interest in politics and that he had named one of his sons, Gladstone, provides clear evidence that he was of a radical disposition. His son later explained the circumstances,

> Gladstone was the Prime Minister in 1890 (1892) for the last time. He was very old but he hadn't lost his popularity at the time I was born. And my grandfather, he was a Liberal you see and he went to the Liberal Club and they had Gladstone's photograph there. He appealed with mi father (for me) to be called Gladstone and that was why I was called Gladstone. It wasn't my father's choice. He didn't mind you know.

As was the case for many skilled working men of the later Victorian era, David Mathers who had been born in 1860, became disillusioned with the Liberal Party and this was especially so in those areas such as West Yorkshire where Liberalism was strong and where the mill owners comprised the local Liberal hierarchy. Such was the case in Skelmanthorpe. Gladstone recalls, 'I remember my father saying that he had given up voting for H J Wilson because when he got to the House of Commons he simply toed the party line. My father's objection to H J Wilson at that particular time, he was advocating things in the constituency, things that when he went there (the Commons) he couldn't put into operation because he simply accepted the whip'.

Wilson was a successful industrialist from Sheffield with a reputation of being an advanced Liberal and was very popular in the Holmfirth Constituency. He opposed the Boer War, advocated land nationalisation and an eight-hour day for the workers. But David Mathers saw through Wilson's inability to support these ideas in Parliament and switched his vote to the emerging Labour candidates and indeed eventually joining the Labour Party. According to his son, he was the first person in the village to take Keir Hardie's weekly newspaper, *Labour Leader*, which he read avidly each and every week.

David Mathers was always very keen that his son should improve himself at work as might have been expected from a radical, skilled Victorian working man. In turn the young man showed ability and began to take an interest in the design aspect of the trade with the result that by the age of nineteen he transferred to become a handloom pattern weaver at the larger mill of Fred Eastwood's in Huddersfield. He remained there for two years learning the trade during which time he began to appreciate the need for trade unions.

On the outbreak of the First World War in 1914, Gladstone moved back to the Shepley Warehouse where he helped form of branch of the National Union of Textile Workers, becoming secretary. Although he opposed the war from its inception, the company was prepared to accept him as an employee. As he commented many years later, 'We always said, and I think it was absolutely correct, the Tory employers of labour were always more broadminded and tolerant than the Liberals in the Huddersfield area' - it was certainly so in Skelmanthorpe.

Gladstone had left school and began his working life in a village where the influence of the church was still strong. In addition to the Anglican Church there were three Methodist churches, the Wesleyan, Reform Wesleyan and Primitive. The radical nature of the non-conformist churches chimed with the radical nature of many of the inhabitants' politics.

Gladstone maintained that the chapels and churches,

> ...made the life of the village, not the pubs. Those who were going to the pubs in those days were those who were going to get drunk. The activities of the village were in the churches, they were even producing plays, you see, and variety concerts on Saturday evenings and parties on Saturday nights, and during the week there was always something going off. I've never known my father connected with the church but my mother was and my grandmother but he was never connected to the church but I think the church would have an influence on him as a lad, in his younger days.

There was a strong social aspect to the attendance at the Methodist chapels. The Wesleyan or Central, was attended by the mill-owners and referred to as the 'posh chapel'. The Primitive Methodists in Pilling Lane represented the other extreme. The Wesleyan congregation tended to be Liberals whilst the Primitive Methodists favoured the emerging Labour Party. Once again Gladstone observed, 'A working class element, absolutely. I should say 100 per cent, I can't think of anybody but working class people connected with the Primitives and also the Wesleyan Reform Chapel'.

The young man began attending the Wesleyan Reform Chapel with his mother and grandmother. For some inexplicable reason, as a 'lad rather than as a young man' he left to join the Wesleyan Methodists, the 'posh' chapel of the mill owners!

> Yes, but you see I didn't understand how these things worked. It was strange. I was connected to the chapel and I was interested in theology, local preaching, etc. and there were certain people who did everything possible to press me to go in, even with the prospect of going in for the ministry. When I was more mature you know and reflected things, I have often wondered why in the world did I join up with the Central Methodist Church. I became a local preacher in the Wesleyan Church.

As Gladstone was maturing he continued with his interest in religion and started to inject a socialist tone into his message. He began to develop political and social consciousness which in turn inter-related with his Christian beliefs. 'As a lad interested in religion, I started being interested in politics and right from a lad, sixteen, seventeen and eighteen years of age, I believed that preachers, local preachers and ministers at that particular time should preach a social gospel as well as individual salvation gospel'.

On one occasion, the young man was invited to preach at his local Wesleyan Church in the village which led to considerable consternation. 'I remember preaching a sermon on bearing one another's burdens and the teachings of Christ you see and it was real Christian socialism'. The mill owner's wife, Mrs Field, took exception and complained of Gladstone, 'He was a grand lad and I was only 18 or 19 years old but she says he was a socialist. You see and my socialism - I joined the Labour

Party because of my Christian socialism. Definitely'. After that his card was marked and in the years following he was to suffer further criticism from the mill owner himself, Thomas Field, for his political and religious opinions during World War I.

When war broke out, Gladstone was living with his parents in the village, working in nearby Shepley at Armitages as a weaver, had become secretary of the trade union branch, continued to act as a lay-preacher in the Methodist Church and was becoming increasingly political. It was hardly surprising that he opposed the war.

He described the situation in his own words,

> At that particular time, I was interested in new religious ideas very early in life and I was influenced by Dr Boland and Dr J E Rattenbury who were out-and-out pacifists. Long before the war I started to entertain pacifist beliefs in opposition to the established view The war broke out and I had no hesitation whatsoever at that particular time as I was reading the literature; the combined influence of the church and the pamphlets I was reading of the ILP and particularly the weekly edition of the *Labour Leader*. There was no hesitation whatsoever in opposing the war. And then right at the beginning, the formation of the No-Conscription Fellowship in Huddersfield. Then as soon as I heard about it I went up to Huddersfield and joined.

During this early period volunteers enlisted in the army in their droves, to grab a bit of glory, smash the Huns and be 'back home for Christmas'. Of course it wasn't anything like that and the war dragged on with casualties mounting daily. Stalemate was reached on the Western Front with the volunteer soldiers trapped in trenches before going 'over the top' with thousands being mown down by the German machine guns. It came as no surprise that the generals wanted more soldiers but the volunteers began to dry up. The campaign to introduce conscription developed and in January 1916, the Military Service Act became law.

Until then, Gladstone and those who thought like him campaigned against the war, met with considerable opprobrium and planned their strategy if conscription were to be introduced. He had continued to work in Shepley alongside his father until he received his call-up papers in early

1916 when the firm told him that they could no longer employ him. He became unemployed and was forced to rely on his parents to keep him.

He was fortunate that there was some opposition to the war amongst the inhabitants of Skelmanthorpe as was the case in certain of the other villages around Huddersfield. This however was in reality still very much a minority point of view. The non-conformist religious tradition had been reinforced by the propaganda work of the ILP over the more recent years. A great many of the national propagandists had spoken in the vicinity and had been supplemented by regional socialist leaders such as Arthur Gardiner and Wilfrid Whiteley. These latter two were also well-known opponents of the war and worked incessantly to get their point of view across.

Gladstone with his background and intelligence became the leader of the conscientious objectors in the village. He was instrumental in the formation of the branch of the No-Conscription Fellowship in Skelmanthorpe with over forty members. Indeed later he gave explicit indication of the extent of support when he recalled, 'I was addressing a meeting at the Working Men's Club right early on you know, and we'd between forty and fifty names given who were going to oppose the war and stand as COs. The ILP was exercising a big influence at that time you know, it was chiefly the ILP, Harry Senior and a person called Ben Morley'.

Perhaps surprisingly given the jingoistic mood pervading the country at the time, the Military Service Act of 1916 had an enlightened clause which allowed individuals who, on grounds of conscience, felt unable to fight, to be exempted from military service. This exemption process was somewhat cumbersome and involved a series of tribunals at both local and sub-regional level which in turn were supplemented by appeal tribunals.

There were 2086 tribunals established at local level which were supplemented by 83 appeal tribunals based on wider local government communities where the local decisions were challenged. Local authority chairs or mayors generally convened the local tribunals and often took the chair. Councillors formed the bulk of the membership but they were on occasions supplemented by trade unions representatives. In addition a representative of the military was compulsory and his task was to make the case why individuals should be conscripted.

Only a very small percentage of cases coming before the local tribunals were based on conscientious objection to taking up arms. The majority of cases were why individuals should not be conscripted on grounds of medical unfitness, business needs or work of national importance.

Unfortunately sections of the Act were loosely drafted which caused great consternation to most of the COs. In particular the critical clause affecting COs read,

> Any certificate of exemption may be absolute, conditional, or temporary, as the authority by whom it was granted think best suited to the case, and also in the case of an application on conscientious grounds, may take the form of an exemption from combatant service only, or may be conditional on the application being engaged in some work which in the opinion of the Tribunal dealing with the case is of national importance… (Section 2 (3)).

The drafting of this section led to great confusion. The intention of the Act was to offer temporary, conditional or absolute exemption to COs. Furthermore there was to be an additional option of recommending the individual to non-combatant service in the army.

Unfortunately for the COs many of the local and appeal tribunals decided that the only option available to them was to recommend non-combatant service or not.

Gladstone initially appeared before the Skelmanthorpe Local Tribunal, as the following month did his eldest brother Haydn who was seven years his senior. Much to Gladstone's chagrin, their claims for complete exemption however failed and they were both granted non-combatant service which meant in simple terms, they had to enlist in the army but they would not be expected to use a gun. As was the normal practice, the local tribunal was composed largely of local councillors and supplemented with a military representative. The chairman was a local Methodist preacher. Gladstone made his appeal for exemption principally on grounds of religion which was underpinned with his socialist convictions. The Methodist chairman remained unimpressed and the young man's objections on grounds of conscience were only partially agreed.

Gladstone felt very strongly that the members of the Skelmanthorpe Tribunal misunderstood what powers they actually had, believing they could only offer non-combatant service. Following his appearance before the tribunal he sought out the individual members and argued vehemently that they actually had much greater options than they realised but to no avail. In reality, given the jingoist mood sweeping the country, the tribunal members were quite content to believe in their limited options.

Following the tribunal, Gladstone had to wait a little time before he received his call-up papers from the army which, as he refused to accept non-combatant service, when they did arrive he simply ignored.

Eventually, towards midnight on the 20 July 1916, the policemen from the neighbouring village of Denby Dale knocked on his front door and got him out of bed. He was taken to the local police station at Scissett where,

> I spent the night in the local police cell. I shan't forget that because they could have fetched me the following morning just as well. I didn't sleep of course, naturally, and in the early morning I was given the few slices of bread and a pot of tea. The policeman from Denby came and took me by train from Denby Dale station and I was put in a cell at Barnsley police station…I spent a night there with two drunken men, they were sober before morning. And I always remember one had a wooden leg, always remember that, I think it was one of the worst nights I ever had in my life…They were rough people but they weren't hostile to me, not nasty in any way whatsoever whether they understood the position or not.

On the morning of the 22 July, he was handed over to the military authorities who took him by train to Halifax Barracks. He was assigned to the 4th Northern Company of the Non-Combatant Corps. There, with other COs, he was paraded in front of the soldiers. 'They did everything possible to put me into 'khaki'. They didn't use physical force, not real physical force. I wasn't hurt in any way whatsoever and I was still in civilian clothes'. His military records also show that he 'refuses medical examination'. By these actions he was demonstrating to the army authorities that he didn't accept their jurisdiction.

From Halifax he was taken by train to Richmond Castle in North Yorkshire where he met up with a number of other COs whom he had known from the Huddersfield area and they were able to give him further advice. They were all kept within the partially-ruined castle walls and allocated cells but they had considerable freedom within the castle, moving about freely and exchanging information. He was advised by the older hands that he should put on the 'khaki' which he did.

Soon after Gladstone arrived and been allocated his cell, he discovered he had a new neighbour in the adjoining cell. The heating pipes at the base of the external walls had been removed and the prisoners were able to communicate through the resultant hole in the thick stone walls where the pipes had once been. His new neighbour was John Charles Beaumont who was a fellow socialist from a village of Hepworth in a neighbouring valley to Skelmanthorpe. John had not put on 'khaki' but Gladstone persuaded him to do so, placing himself in the same situation as the majority of COs.

They spent almost two weeks at Richmond during which time the officers and NCOs tried to persuade them to accept non-combatant service. Gladstone recounted how the captain spent hours arguing the Christian case for war. Eventually he asked them to obey the command to join the army as non-combatant forces but they all flatly refused. Finally, the officer lost his temper and began shouting and yelling at them and threatening all sorts of retribution. In groups of eight, the COs were brought before the captain in front of the soldiers lined-up on parade. The sentences were fairly standardised with Gladstone being given 112 days hard labour to be served at Durham Prison for 'refusing to obey a lawful order given by his superior officer'. The stay at Richmond had been fairly benign for the army's strategy was to show a kindly face in the hope of persuading the COs to reconsider their positions and join the army. There was no physical ill-treatment by the army but prior to Gladstone going to Richmond some other COs had suffered maltreatment.

This had not been directly at the hands of the soldiers but by the general public. The COs had been taken out onto the streets of Richmond, a garrison town with a long military tradition, to show the local inhabitants what type of men were refusing to fight for their country. The general public didn't like the COs, a number of whom were somewhat maltreated but not severely so.

One rule which the army insisted upon was that he COs were not permitted to communicate with anyone in the outside world. As Gladstone described however, by an ingenious plan they found a way round this restriction,

> We all wrote a letter and a person called Lawson had a young lady came too. We couldn't have visitors but some way he had got a letter out so that a visitor could come to the castle's walls. At one end of the castle grounds there was a deep drop on to the road that went round the castle. We all wrote a letter and put it in one envelope and Lawson managed to throw this letter down to his young lady. All our friends and relatives received a letter from her.

He was transferred to Durham on 4 August 1916 where the COs had to share the prison with regular criminals. He began almost four months of solitary confinement when the only time he could chat with his fellow prisoners was when they were emptying their slops each morning or undertaking their daily exercise. Then they exchanged any gossip.

There he found the conditions far from comfortable. Food he described as, 'it was poor, really poor...It was porridge in the morning and about two ounces of very brown bread. One meal during the day was two ounces of fatty bacon. Bread and baked beans one day and porridge at night. Plenty of water to drink'.

The warders were 'not too bad' and one even showed himself eventually to be sympathetic. Apparently this became apparent when the COs were being transferred to Wormwood Scrubs in London to appear before the Central Appeals Tribunal, 'We were taken from Durham prison by wagonette to Durham Station and there was one of the warders, off duty at that particular time, and he met us and shook hands with one or two and wished us well'.

There was one incident which became part of the folklore amongst the COs which has been corroborated from various sources which Gladstone described with relish,

> We had two church services on Sunday and one during the week and the governor's daughter played the organ for these services. During the time I was there the governor had his fortnight holiday. The chief warder took charge and he had nobody to play the organ. A person from Mirfield or Batley was a good musician and

he could play the organ, a CO and he volunteered to play the organ and he did for two Sundays. On the last occasion he suddenly struck up the Red Flag. Then one started singing and then another until we were all singing the Red Flag…The warders were yelling at us to stop. They were doing everything to stop us but they could not stop us.

It was following that incident that Gladstone travelled down to the Central Appeal Tribunal at Wormwood Scrubs where he appeared in front of three Peers. Apparently they attended not singly but in groups of two or three. Although most of the pleas were made on moral or religious grounds there was one individual with him who argued his case on economic grounds. He told the tribunal that he wasn't opposed to war. He believed in the class war and the next battle would be between the forces of socialism and those of capitalism. Perhaps not surprisingly his appeal was rejected!

As it happened, that visit to the Central Appeal on 31 August 1916 proved very successful for Gladstone and many of his fellow COs. It found that he was genuine and deemed him as Class A (Genuine). Those like Gladstone who were deemed to be genuine were over time transferred to work-centres usually attached to prisons.

In due course he was offered a place at Wakefield Work Centre, only a dozen or so miles from his home, on 28 February 1917 where he found the conditions there were much more congenial than Durham Prison. Gladstone suspected the governor of being a Quaker and he and the staff treated the COs in a much more humane manner. An attempt was made to match up their civilian skills with what the authorities needed and Gladstone began working on the looms again, weaving prison clothes - nothing to do with the war effort.

In many respects the COs were allowed to organise their own lives inside the centres. They were permitted a great deal of freedom and in Wakefield numerous societies were formed with many of the highly educated COs giving lectures and talks. Such was the freedom that there were reports of a branch of the ILP being formed in the work centre (*Labour Leader*, 30 November 1916). It was a fascinating time which Gladstone described as his university,

That was really our university for a while. It really was. It was very good but there was always the war. We were always discussing the war and then there was the schools when we got together planning for the future. There was a lot of that being done by those who were socialists. Not particularly those narrow-minded Christians. They weren't interested. They never came to those classes on what to do after the war, how to develop things, what to be interested in, how to get in touch with local authorities and one thing and another. In fact at that particular time, there were those few who when we got out, kept in contact with one another and formed some form of communal life same as they did at Town End. It was formed but it came to nothing. It was to a certain extent a valuable time and I am convinced that a lot of people hadn't seriously looked into things; we'll say industrial matters and taking part in community life. I think it resulted in a lot of them being interested more than they ever were.

There were approximately 400 COs at Wakefield with the majority being socialists, many of them Christian Socialists and scores of photographs remain of the COs in the work-centre at both work and leisure. They received some payment, up to three shillings (15p) a week as wages for their work. There was a library and they could have as many books as they wished. From the time they moved in, they were permitted to return home at weekends - a privilege Gladstone was easily able to make use of.

There was one unpalatable experience which Gladstone never forgot. As he explained,

> One Monday morning Gilbert (the governor) had me in his office along with the other Skelmanthorpe COs. He said 'I have received a letter signed by Thomas Field, chairman of the council, saying that at weekends you are doing propaganda work and asking for you and others not to be allowed to come out of the Wakefield Centre'. However we told him we didn't have time to do propaganda work as we were simply visiting our friends and our relatives.

Gladstone never forgave Thomas Field, the principal mill owner locally and the patron of the Central Methodist Chapel where he himself was a lay preacher, for being so mean-spirited and went so far as to suggest that Field himself wasn't much older than they were and it was strange that he hadn't been called up for military service. Later when his brother Harold, was elected a councillor he learned that the letter of complaint although purporting to be on official council business had not been approved by the council.

After the rigours and hardship of army barracks and civilian prison, Wakefield Work Centre was much appreciated by the COs. The staff were much more amenable with a governor who was understanding. The regime was tolerant and with the inmates being drawn from many diverse social backgrounds, most of the COs were able to make the most of the experience.

There were four brothers in the Mather family. The eldest brother, Haydn, was also a CO and followed an almost identical path to Gladstone. Granted the non-combatant corps option at the Skelmanthorpe Local Tribunal, lost his appeal in Huddersfield, ignored his call-up papers and was arrested. He was taken to Halifax Barracks where the army tried unsuccessfully to enlist him into the 5th Northern NCC. From Halifax he was transferred to 11 South Staffordshire Regiments camp at Rugeley where, on 31 August 1916, he was court mar-shalled and sentenced to two years hard labour in Winsome Green Prison which was later commuted to one year. On 21 September 1916 he appeared before the Central Tribunal in Wormwood Scrubs and deemed a Class A (Genuine) CO and eventually joined Gladstone at Wakefield Work Centre in 1917.

Harold, five years older than Gladstone, had lost his job as a textile worker in a local mill in the early years of the War and had found work on a nearby farm. He too applied to the local Tribunal for exemption as a CO and as he was employed as a farm worker, he was excused military service as this was regarded as an essential job. As well having very strong socialist views like his younger brother, Harold was also deeply interest-ed in theological and religious matters. Christianity was an integral part of his socialist convictions and on his death he left scores of theology books.

The youngest brother Sydney, who was three years Gladstone's junior and very close to him, was the exception, joining the local West Riding Regiment, the Duke of Wellington's, and seeing active service in Flanders and France. He was killed at Arras on 3 May 1917 and is buried in Faubourg-d'Amiens Cemetery in Arras.

Sydney's service in the army and subsequent loss, does serve to emphasise how divisive World War One was. In the literally scores of talks with Gladstone, he only once mentioned Sydney. His service in the army was only discovered long after Gladstone's death. One can only speculate on the reasons why Sydney was rarely mentioned but it was a surprise to find he had joined the army to fight in a war his three brothers so vehemently opposed.

Haydn was not to live to build his political dream. He caught the Spanish 'Flu and like so many other young men died from it. This strain of influenza particularly targeted fit young people and more individuals died from it than lost their lives in World War One. Thus Alice Mathers lost two of her four sons in the war and the family always maintained she died prematurely broken hearted. On her tombstone, there is reference to both Haydn and Sydney.

When Gladstone eventually returned home after the war in 1919, he faced the problem of finding a job. Generally he claimed the hostility to himself and his fellow COs was not too strong in the village.

> We were opposed to a certain extent but Skelmanthorpe was divided and in the main I was treated very, very well. There were elements that were opposed to me and there were any amount of people who wouldn't speak to me for a long time but because of my beliefs at the time, I didn't retaliate. In the end, even those who had been opposed to me, started talking to me. I think that within twenty years at any rate there wouldn't be anybody who was refusing to talk to me. I was regarded as the leader of the Skelmanthorpe COs you see, but during the whole of that time we were sympathetically dealt with even by those who were opposing us.

It was difficult for COs to find work. Many employers flatly refused to take them back after the war. Norton's, Edwin Field's and Jackson's were notoriously difficult according to Gladstone. He went on to explain his experiences,

> I tried to get a job at Learoyd's on Leeds Road (Huddersfield) and

I thought I was getting the job and then at the end they started asking me what I'd been doing and so forth and they said they couldn't set me on. Meanwhile my uncle had got to a place at Newsome, Taylor and Littlewoods, so I wrote and had an interview with them and they set me on as a hand loom pattern maker, But in the meantime some way or other, they got to know what I'd been doing, what I'd been standing for and I received a letter saying I couldn't continue with the job.

A few of us at Wakefield heard that T W Broadbent's was prepared to give the COs just the same chance as anybody else. He hadn't been opposing the war but he had been supporting the COs during the war you see and I and another got on at T W Broadbent's. We started working in the storeroom. We had the sympathy of the employer and not so much sympathy from those who were working; not too bad, there was two of us. We exercised an influence and somehow we came through alright but we had a certain amount of opposition. In some instances (in Huddersfield) there were those who refused to work with COs you know after the war. But they never attempted to say that they wouldn't work with us. In fact I got married whilst I was there and they bought me a handsome present so I must have got on all right with them.

In the summer of 1921 he married Annie Dyson at the Congregational Church in nearby Shelley. They soon had a son who was named after his lost brother Haydn but their joy was short-lived for the baby died prematurely and they had no further family. Meanwhile, politically he had become very active in the local Labour party, becoming its secretary. He was finding travelling to work in Huddersfield somewhat tiresome and eventually managed to find a job locally at Herbert Firth's of Shepley which was within walking distance. Whilst he was there he helped form a branch of the union and recruited many members but always only a minority.

From there he moved to Cairn Stewart's where he found the atmosphere even more congenial but this may simply have been as the result of the passage of time since the end of hostilities. In politics the mood had changed quickly during those years. In the General Election of 1918 the Labour MPs who had been opposed to the war lost their seats, including Ramsay MacDonald and Philip Snowden, but by the early 1920s almost all had been returned again to the House of Commons.

Whilst even at the local level, Harold, Gladstone's older brother who was well-known for his anti-war views and been granted exemption from joining the army, had won a seat on Skelmanthorpe Urban District Council in 1919. As to prove this wasn't a flash in the pan, he remained on the council for thirty-nine years until his death in January 1958.

The housing shortage which caused so much consternation to the soldiers returning to 'the land fit for heroes' was even more problematic for former COs. They faced prejudice as well as the shortage of houses. Gladstone was no exception. Initially, he had returned to live at home with his father and then following his marriage he moved in with his in-laws whilst searching for a home of his own - always in vain. Eventually, it was his brother Harold who came to his rescue.

Harold had always been keen on politics and never forgot that in the early years of the War, he had lost his job as a weaver in the textile industry on account of his views on the War. Thus when he was elected to the local council in 1919 he realised it would be difficult for him to remain an effective Labour councillor whilst dependent on the whim or prejudice of some employer. The only solution was to become self-employed when he could determine his own work schedule. This was a path which had been followed by many of the earlier Labour pioneers and councillors.

With this in mind, he joined his Uncle George and bought some land in Skelmanthorpe on which they established a poultry farm. Whilst the poultry farm was being built up they both continued working in textiles until such time it could provide Harold with a living. In 1925, he felt able to give Gladstone a small plot of land upon which he built a two-bedroomed bungalow for himself and Annie. He lived there for almost sixty years.

Eventually the venture prospered and Gladstone joined his brother on the poultry farm and together they gradually built up a successful business. Not only did they market chickens for eating but they also developed regular rounds delivering eggs in neighbouring towns such as Huddersfield and Wakefield.

Initially to do this they bought a motor-bike and sidecar and became a regular sight in the district, with Gladstone riding the bike, Harold behind on the pillion and the sidecar crammed with eggs. In the 1930s, as the business expanded they swapped their motor cycle for a Singer car but when petrol was rationed in the early years of World War Two, this part of the business proved impossible. The egg delivery rounds failed but local people still came to the farm for their eggs and the brothers diversified into raising day-old chicks which again proved to be a very successful enterprise.

Throughout these years, Harold continued with his council work whilst Gladstone worked hard behind the scenes supporting Harold both in their business and party work. He always maintained he was essentially always working for the Labour Party locally, holding many of the local offices. Meanwhile Harold emerged over the years as the leading local Labour councillor on both Skelmanthorpe and then Denby Dale UDCs and his record showed how highly he was regarded. In particular he was proud as chair of the Housing Committee in the years following the Second World War when he struggled to re-house the men and women who had returned from the hostilities. It was a stressful period but he masterminded plans to build scores of houses in the locality and eventually a street was named in his honour, Matherville.

On Harold's sixty-fifth birthday in 1953, it was decided to wind-up the poultry business. Gladstone, who was five years younger returned to work in the textile industry at Armitage's at Shepley. It had been a happy and successful time for the brothers and Harold in particular was able to devote even more of his time to his civic duties as a councillor and a Justice of the Peace.

In the 1930s, Gladstone's family house proved invaluable to the local Labour Party. In those years, there were many visiting speakers and the local parties had little money. Thus it was the custom that the speakers were put up in the homes of local activists. Gladstone's house may not have been palatial but it was much better than most of the houses of Labour Party members. Thus a galaxy of visitors stayed with the couple and on occasions they would even give up their own bedroom for the speakers and move into the homes of relatives.

One particular visitor who visited the village on at least two occasions was Katherine St John Conway, or Katherine Bruce Glasier as she became on her marriage. She was a particularly attractive woman and a brilliant speaker and propagandist and she stayed at the bungalow, becoming a warm favourite of the family. She had lost her husband to cancer and her son Glen in a tragic accident. Her socialism was heavily interlinked with Christianity which struck a resonant chord with the Mathers family.

Following Annie's death, right up until the 1980s, Gladstone remained active in the local Labour Party. His politics and his religion remained intertwined to the end; each dependent on the other. He was quite explicit you couldn't be a Christian without being a socialist.

Outlining his lifetime beliefs in the mid-1970s, he continued to emphasise the importance of Christianity and Socialism,

> I still believe. And that's the reason why, that for a long period I was outside the church and I didn't go to church. I felt as though the Labour movement was doing the work of the church and the church wasn't being involved in the rights of the people as it ought to have. But in later years, I came to this conclusion, whilst we weren't active enough in the community, that after all was retaining the great idealistic Christian principle that in the end, it would have to be put into operation if the world is going to improve. And to that end I'm disillusioned because I'm afraid the churches are going back to the individualistic gospel, salvation by faith, the old way that I have repudiated a long long time ago and never accepted; even when I was seventeen years of age I never accepted. Well they're going back to that to a certain extent, ours isn't, it preaches the individual gospel of course but it's preaching the social gospel as well.

Gladstone Mathers died in his beloved Skelmanthorpe on 17 October 1984 at the age of ninety-one. To the very end, his faith in Christianity and Socialism remained undiminished and he always remained firm in the belief of the ultimate goodness of people.

Quotations of Gladstone Mathers from interviews with David Clark on 31 October 1974, 27 March 1975, 19 May 1977 and 29 December 1977.

6

John Charles Beaumont
1888-1979

On the wall of my study hangs a watercolour print of probably the best known Liberal Prime Minister, W E Gladstone and his wife taking afternoon tea at Hawarden Castle. It is not of any value to anyone but myself. It was a gift from a lifelong Labour activist, John Charles Beaumont, and exemplified the importance of radical Liberalism in the later years of the nineteenth century which by its failure to understand the social changes taking place in industrial Britain, was crucial to the successful emergence of the Labour Party. John himself, being born in 1888, had never been a Liberal but his father had until his conversion to Labour.

I regarded John as a wise friend with so many years of political experience. He was still in the house in Towngate, Hepworth where he had lived for over seventy years. Visits to his home were sheer joy, not only to talk with John but also to visit his 'library'. He lived and slept on the ground floor whilst the two upstairs bedrooms were lined from floor to ceiling with books. He considered himself as only an ordinary working man but he was exceedingly well-read and loved his books. He read avidly, not only politics but also philosophy, religion, history and wider. He took delight in showing me Ruskin's or Carlyle's works in addition to the more obscure local authors who wrote about the surrounding Yorkshire Pennine area. I too loved his books and much appreciated his breadth and wealth of knowledge.

He was always urging me to take some of his books then one day, he took the picture of Gladstone off his living-room wall, and insisted that I took it. He knew it would be a reminder to me of his lifelong commitment to Labour politics which he had so enthusiastically and lastingly embraced following the failure of even the greatest Liberal in his eyes, WE Gladstone.

John was born on tenth February 1888 in the village of Hepworth which nestles 1000 feet in the Yorkshire Pennines. Below, across the valley, runs the direct road from Huddersfield to Sheffield but in the village itself the streets are winding, narrow and steep with John's house being right in the centre. In the twenty-first century it has seen many new houses being built and has become a very desirable village in which to live.

This is a far-cry from the days at the end of the nineteenth century or most of the twentieth, when it was decidedly a working class community. When John was born most of the work was in either the wool textiles or mining, with his father working in textiles. Immediately to the south of the village, over the water table in the next valley, were a number of coal mines from where ganister was also extracted to be used in the neighbouring brick making plant.

The district had been in the administrative County of the West Riding of Yorkshire and in the Parliamentary Constituency reforms of 1885, it became part of the newly created Holmfirth Division where it remained until the constituency's abolition in 1918 when it was transferred to the Colne Valley.

Hepworth, along with the neighbouring parishes of Fulstone and Scholes, was part of New Mill Urban District Council until it was merged in 1938 to form the larger Holmfirth UDC which in turn was abolished in 1974 becoming part of Kirklees Metropolitan District Council.

The south Pennine districts of Yorkshire had somewhat of a reputation of favouring radical politics and Holmfirth was no exception. The first MP was a Sheffield industrialist, H J Wilson who was regarded as an advanced Liberal. He embraced all the traditional radical issues, non-conformity, temperance, Irish Home Rule, internationalism, dis-establishment of the Church of England and the eight hour day. He comfortably retained the seat until his resignation on grounds of ill-health in 1912. He was succeeded at the by-election by a similar radical Liberal, Sydney Arnold. He in turn was to leave the Liberals, join the Labour Party in 1922 and two years later was ennobled as Baron Arnold and served in the First Labour Government as Under-Secretary of State for Colonies and then later as Paymaster General from 1929-31.

One of Wilson's sons, Cecil Henry, became the Labour MP for

Sheffield Attercliffe in 1922 and held the seat, with a break in 1931, until 1944. But this would have been a step too far for his father who although undoubtedly of radical views, found it difficult to accept socialism or the Labour Party. He was very comfortable with, and indeed campaigned for, Lib-Lab MPs. Early in his career this earned him a great deal of political support from the Yorkshire miners whose union, the YMA, came to an agreement for some of their leaders to stand as Lib-Lab MPs. In 1908 however, all this changed when the miners of the YMA voted to support the Labour Party and then their Lib-Lab MPs switched to Labour.

Already an increasing number of younger miners were supporting the ILP and as early as the 1910 General Election, a number of Labour supporters locally determined to test their support at the ballot box. They persuaded William Pickles, an activist in the painters' union and a Huddersfield Labour councillor, to stand but with a somewhat disappointing result as he attracted 1643 votes or 14.9 per cent. Whilst they had hoped for a higher vote it was to be a good base for future contests. Amongst those campaigning in that election was John Beaumont and his other colleagues from the New Mill ILP.

Two years later, they were on the streets once again in a Parliamentary by-election when an ILP activist and well-known YMA member, Willie Lunn was the Labour candidate and he fared very much better. He remained third but only by a whisker, almost doubling the Labour vote with 3195 votes or 28.2 per cent. In a sense this was the crucial contest when Labour established itself as the credible force in the constituency.

John Beaumont left Hepworth Primary School when he was thirteen and began work in the brickworks which were part of the industrial complex which included coal mines, a couple of miles south of his home. This involved a walk over the moorland tracks and a climb of 400 feet to the head of the valley. In inclement weather, for which this part of Yorkshire is renowned especially in winter, it would have been a challenging experience for the young worker.

His daily route would take him past the remote Barnside Farm, where ten years later a young orphan would be brought to work down the local pit. That young boy was Joe Driver and later he was to be a fellow member of John's in the ILP at New Mill and a life-long member of the Labour Party. If John even felt his early life in the brickworks was hard, he would have conceded Joe's in the pit at the age of thirteen was even tougher.

In Joe Driver's own words over sixty years later,

> I went to school at Outlane (Huddersfield) until I was thirteen then a farmer from Barnside, Victoria (near Hepworth) came for me. He wanted me for the farm and the pit. A great many of we orphan boys ended up in the pits. I was going to school at Outlane on the Monday and on the Tuesday morning I was down the pit. I shall never forget that first morning at Crow Edge Colliery above Holmfirth. I was so small I couldn't reach the bars in the cage. One of the big miners picked me up.
>
> The farmer was a good chap but he stuck to the rules. I gave him my wages. As orphan girls and boys we were tied until the girls were sixteen and the boys, eighteen. When I was eighteen, I wanted to leave but my landlady wanted £2 from me. She said this was £1 to leave and another £1 for the first week I had stayed with them when I went there in 1911.
>
> I got 10 pence a day when I first started. I was very small but gradually as I got stronger I took on another collier and then got 2 shillings a day and then I got to where I was earning 4 shillings a day. It was hard work though, tramming.
>
> When I was seventeen and a half, they gave me my picks and I was attached to a collier. I was with him six months and then I was fully blown. We were working in the Halifax Hard Seam which was 2 foot 4 inches thick and I was paid 30 shillings. When I finished with the collier and went on my own I got £2 per week.
>
> It was only a little pit. About 200 yards and you were at the bottom and there were about 80 colliers. There was ganister under the coal and this was used in the brick making process. In addition to the Hepworth Pit at Crow Edge there was also another one, a day hole. I was moved to it for a while when they were short of trammers. I went back to Hepworth in 1916. At Crow Edge, we were so well organised that I couldn't start work there when I was thirteen until I joined the union. The manager daren't take us on unless we were.

When Joe began working at the pit, John Beaumont was well established at the adjoining brickworks which were situated in the same industrial complex. Indeed the coal from the Crow Edge Mine was of poor quality and used primarily to provide power in the brickworks with any surplus being sold to the local mills. He was eleven when he began at the brickworks and described the work graphically,

> I was carrying bricks off for some women - three women came from Staffordshire, it were a right brick spot in Staffordshire. I was only eleven and it was a hard job for a young lad - you were labouring. They were fairly heavy those bricks and they made these bricks and emptied them onto some pallets. Then we'd pick them up and carried them to the end of the shed. It was a long way to go in the morning and we got nearer, up to the night. The morning after we went in at 7 o'clock and picked up all these bricks - they were set then.
>
> I was only there twelve months then I moved to another job at Tinkers and then in a year or two I started mixing. I was on the stage with a long pug mill, you know, where the clay came through and turn your water on and making bricks. I made about 9000 a day and then they got a big pug mill from mixing the clay for the pipes...it was a right easy job, I'd only to have my hand on the water tap, regulate it and I'd been mixing with the machine for ten years and I could tell how the clay was the way it was throwing it over.

John had become a skilled member of the workforce but when World War I began in 1914, he was made redundant. Unable to find work he spent all that summer at home until he got another job locally, building the dam at the new Greaves Reservoir at Hade Edge.

> It were dirty you know, they hadn't got a waterway or anything, sticking to your boots. It were hard sport and all. It were harder spot than brickworks. And when it rained we went into the cabin and he always marked it out, the foreman; how long we'd been stopped. It were all taken off. I stayed there 'til it got bad, in the middle of winter.

He then found work labouring at Shelley Woollen Mill where he stayed for a short period. By 1914, John had become very active in the local ILP, was a committee member of the union at the brickworks and was well-known for his strongly held political views. In particular he had formed strong anti-war opinions and when conscription was introduced in January 1916 he decided he would refuse to fight and apply to be a conscientious objector.

> I left the Ford Mill 'cos I knew the police were going to fetch me. I'd a bit of straightening up to do at home...Then the war cropped up, and you see with being brought up in the ILP, I was anti-war. Most of the COs round this district were ILPers and a lot worked at Sidney Mill.

John appeared before the Military Service Tribunal at Huddersfield on 12 May 1916 claiming exemption from military service on grounds of conscience and was granted non-combatant service. Interestingly, Gladstone Mathers appeared before the same Tribunal. Towards the end of July, after a short period when he was deemed a fugitive, he found himself again in Gladstone's company at Halifax Barracks as the army attempted to persuade them to accept service in Non Combatant Corps (4th Northern). Then they occupied adjacent cells at Richmond Castle where they again adopted a similar approach, refusing to join the Army and on 4 August 1916 being court-martialled and sentenced to 112 days hard labour, to be served at Durham Prison where Gladstone was also sent.

At Durham, John recalled that all they seemed to get to eat was porridge with water to drink. One of the highlights he remembered vividly, was when the Governor's daughter, who played the prison chapel's organ, went away on holiday and one of the COs volunteered to deputise for her. Then at the end of the final service, he struck up with the chords of the Red Flag which they all joined in the singing, much to the chagrin of the prison warders who went wild, shouting and yelling, as they attempted to restore order, which of course they failed to do until the COs had completed their singing of the socialist anthem. Almost sixty years later in 1974, he still enjoyed regaling me with that memory.

Towards the end of August 1916, he, along with others including

Gladstone Mathers, was taken by train to London and on the 31st, appeared before the Central Appeal Tribunal at Wormwood Scrubs. There he was deemed to be a genuine CO, Class A. After fulfilling his sentence at Durham he was transferred to the Wakefield Work Centre on 18 November 1916 and there he found the conditions to be much more congenial.

Wakefield Work Centre 1918. John Beaumont seated extreme right and Gladstone Mathers second row far left

In the years following their release from Wakefield, Gladstone Mathers and John Beaumont both returned to their home areas and became active in their respective local branches of the Labour Party. However, although only less than ten miles apart, they were in different constituency parties and as such their paths never crossed. Having interviewed them both, I realised that they had served together in prison. Both confirmed this but had never met since they had left the Wakefield Work Centre and I was able to take Gladstone to meet John at Hepworth in autumn 1974 when they spent a great afternoon reminiscing.

After the war, John was more fortunate than some in that he quickly found work. Nevertheless, even his initial efforts met with disappointment. He described his first interview at a Holmfirth textile mill, 'I went into this mill and I could tell he was going to set me on. 'Oh', I says, 'I'd better tell you I'm a CO. I've just come from Wakefield'. 'Oh', he says, 'I think we don't want anyone'.

Happily, he then had two work offers, one at Greaves Reservoir and the other at a mill in Honley but eventually he went back to Hepworth Iron Company where he was set on. Once there, he immediately joined the Gasworkers and General Labourers Union, quickly becoming the branch chairman. In 1921 he 'got stopped again and I went back to my poultry and my gardening'.

By this time John was becoming increasingly active in the Labour Party and was considering running for a seat on the New Mill UDC. He had a large garden and a plot of land by his house where he lived with his mother. Like so many other early Labour activists and councillors he had already experienced the vagaries of being employed and active political- ly and determined to become self-employed. He utilised his house as the village shop and by this means and his poultry and gardening, he was able to earn a living.

John's father, William, had been born in Hepworth and worked as a woollen weaver. In addition to his wife he had four daughters and two sons of whom John was the eldest boy. By the time of the 1911 Census, the eldest daughter was working in the shop based at their home. William had been a Liberal but John proudly boasted he had converted him to Labour. Like so many working men in the area, he had voted for H J Wilson but became disenchanted. In John's own words,

> I used to go to the meetings here. They used to hold their meet-
> ings here. The Liberals and then the Tories and all thy talked
> about, election after election, were free trade and farm prices. That
> were all they talked about. They never did ought. Poverty went on
> just the same. It all reminds me of that story I once heard a Labour
> man tell in New Mill. He used to say how they'd been promising
> working class all these years. He said they had a long stick over a
> donkey's back with a carrot hung down so far off his nose. This
> donkey went after this carrot, riding a fellow around. That's the
> working people - promising them this carrot and they never got it.

The mood however was changing amongst thinking working men who increasingly began to see the Labour Movement meeting their political desires. There had been a flurry of activity in the early 1890s in nearby Colne Valley and Huddersfield. At Honley, a village just a couple of miles down the road from New Mill, a Labour Club had been formed as early as 1891 and it had survived the vicissitudes of the following decade.

As interest in socialism revived in the years following 1900, a group of workingmen from the New Mill district determined to follow the Honley example. They decided to test the water and in the summer months of 1905 held a series of meetings throughout the district. Following successful outdoor meetings in June and July, on 12 August they decided to take the message to outlying villages of Netherthong, Scholes and Wooldale.

Again they found an encouraging response and on 3 September 1905 formally established the New Mill branch of the ILP. The momentum continued and on 5 December they held a public meeting which attracted 5-600 people at which it was announced that the branch had over 100 members. A disused mill on Sude Hill in the village was acquired as the headquarters and it too prospered, attracting many members and visiting speakers. They continued to use the mill as the Labour Hall until eventually moving into a wooden hut nearby.

Amongst the younger members in those early days was John Beaumont who described his own impressions,

> I should join when I was 15 ...Now the New Mill ILP in those days, they were what I call idealists. You know the ILP, more of a religious stamp. I think it was largely built up by local preachers. Nonconformists, that is not church people, and we had speakers from all over. We were up in that old mill and then we had dances and like to make a bit of money. It was a grand room for dancing such a long mill. I suppose the first time I'd gone to a meeting in New Mill, I was struck by the theory. Up to 15, I used to attend chapel. I sort of broke away from it and I got more agnostic.

He was correct in his reference to the preachers. This was confirmed by Herman Barker, the secretary of Holmfirth Divisional Labour Representation Council (LRC) who on 24 July 1907 wrote to Ramsay MacDonald,

> We have a few parsons in the neighbourhood who are supporting us. Graham, curate in charge at Thongsbridge (immediately adja-

cent to New Mill), worked like a horse for Grayson; he is preaching socialism openly every Sunday from the pulpit and advising all to support and join the Labour Party. Turnbull, Vicar of New Mill is on the same track and they are keeping our powerful enemies, who aim at checking the movement by victimisation of our members, in check. When they preach away from their own church they act as our advanced guard and they are using their influence amongst their class to our advantage every time (Labour Party Archives LPGC 17/142).

The ethical appeal of the ILP had considerable resonance in the local Church of England, many of whose vicars were attracted to the Labour cause. Christian Socialism had a strong following in certain circles of the Church around the end of the nineteenth century. The Community of the Resurrection, an Anglican Order based at nearby Mirfield, was in particular involved in this movement and in 1906 formed an organisation called Socialists of the West Riding with many of its incumbents urging support for Labour. However most of the ILP members in the Pennine area of the West Riding would be drawn from the non-conformist churches. Later John experienced a similar phenomenon at the Wakefield Work Centre for COs where there was a large number of practising Christians (Clark, 1981 p.148).

Another miner from Scholes, the adjoining village to Hepworth, Ernest Beever, who was nine years younger than John Beaumont, corroborates his view of New Mill ILP. He had joined in 1915 and explained how he had drifted into politics by way of Primitive Methodism.

> When we joined the Labour Party (New Mill ILP) they were having dances during the First World War and my brother Hubert was a pianist. He had learned to play when he was ten. He played for the dances. Oh they were disgraced - the Methodists. We didn't take a bit of notice. We still went on and considered ourselves as good Methodists as they were.
>
> We were working in the pit (Crow Edge) for about seven shillings a day. I was fond of going out. We'd a bit of land, ten acres, besides working at the pit - poultry and that. We had a few young cows. It was just a hobby like.

We started playing for dances at the Labour Hall, 1914-18. Hubert ended up playing for dances at the Labour Hall. They used to say 'If you're going in for an organist, you can't go on playing for dances at the Labour Rooms'. Well Hubert said, 'if I give up playing for the dances, I'll have to give up my lessons because my mother can't afford to pay for them'.

Ernest Beever was active in the miners' union as chairman of the local branch and remained in the ILP until the Labour Party provided for individual membership after 1918. He recalled,

Arthur Henderson, or somebody, sent us up to fifty cards one night. We were always eager to pay and we were members of the national Labour Party and still several of us paid into the ILP - and I got rid of fifty cards that night.

His father was also a miner and also on the local committee. He was keen to encourage Ernest and Hubert to become active in politics. He took them down as youngsters to hear Victor Grayson as well as the Labour Leader, Keir Hardie,

Oh I was so young and my father was paddling me down the street. My father got hit with a sward (of soil) on the side of the face. They were throwing them at Keir Hardie who was riding on a wagonette.

He remembered too when the suffragettes brought their caravan to Crown Bottom in New Mill where Sylvia Pankhurst held an open-air meeting. The ILP nationally was very supportive of women's suffrage and the two bodies gradually worked closely together in the political arena.

The two Beever brothers went on to become stalwarts of the local Labour Party, both serving as councillors, first on New Mill and then on Holmfirth UDC from the 1930s and for the following three decades. Ernest was the most prominent and was secretary of the local branch and Constituency delegate for many years.

John Beaumont attended the same Keir Hardie meeting in New Mill and retained a vivid memory of it,

> I remember Keir Hardie speaking. I'll tell you where he was stood. There's a shaving shop just below the square in New Mill. There weren't really any motors and only a few horse passengers. I remember him talking; him with a beard and a long coarse pipe. He says, 'Give me a people with a light of knowledge in their eyes, the state of freedom in their souls and the milk of human kindness in their hearts and we will win the war for socialism'. That were a quotation from Keir Hardie. I was impressed by him - fine old chap.

One interesting anecdote about Keir Hardie came from Edna Mosley. She was the daughter of France Littlewood who was a mill owner in Honley and also leader of the local socialists as well as being a Labour councillor. Having a large house meant that visiting dignitaries stayed there including the Labour leader. Edna Mossley attended the village school and her schoolmates were intrigued by Hardie. There was a great deal of prejudice against him and

> There were those who said, 'Oh that dirty old man. I wouldn't have him in the house'. ...He was a delightful person and spotless. I was very young of course in those days and I sneaked into his bed-room, when he was out with father, to see what he wore at night - a beautiful white nightshirt.

Being ten years older than Joe Driver or Ernest Beever, John was active much earlier in the ILP. He acted as sub-secretary for the villages of Hepworth and Scholes and was recognised as the leading socialist in the area. He heard many of the early propagandists and helped in the Colne Valley by-election of 1907 which resulted in Victor Grayson's surprising election victory. Amongst those he heard during those years were Ernest Marklew who was MP for Colne Valley 1935-39, Victor Grayson, Bruce Glasier and his wife Kathleen, John Wheatley and W C Anderson. When asked who was the most impressive, he responded,

As a speaker, Marklew were a grand one, so was Grayson. Possibly Grayson might be the more impressive. He used to tell tales about Ancoats in Manchester. He came from there and he told about the poverty and the state they were living in. Funny thing he disappeared.

In the pre-radio and pre-TV age, newspapers were important for political parties to get across their ideas and policies. John Beaumont read widely and explained,

Robert Blatchford's *Clarion*, I didn't get that so much but I took the *Labour Leader* regularly. Then there was the *Daily Citizen* and then the *Daily Herald*.

Naturally, most of John's political activity in the days before World War I, was in the Constituency. He recalled working in the campaign to get William Pickles elected in the January 1910 General Election and then for Billy Lunn in the 1912 by-election. Lunn was a sound choice for he was a miner from an adjacent constituency and although he did not win, many of the miners in Holmfirth switched their votes to him. He didn't contest the seat again as he was elected as the MP for his home constituency of Rothwell.

The majority of the early activists in the New Mill ILP were textile workers although there were several coal mines in the area and a miners club in the village. The miners' union, the YMA, had traditionally sided with the Liberal Party and indeed a number of their leaders had sat in the Commons as Lib-Lab MPs. Gradually however the younger miners switched their support to the socialist ILP. Billy Lunn was prominent amongst these but then in 1908, the YMA decided, following a ballot of members, to support the newly established Labour Party.

There was some suggestions that at times there was a tension between the miners and other workers. John Beaumont hints at this,

When they formed the Labour Party there was a lot of them (miners), they were Liberals. They called them Lib-Labs and you know they took some getting out. They were Lib-Labs for years after the

Labour Party. You see they had come in as miners' leaders but they were Liberals really.

Herman Barker, secretary of Holmfirth LRC makes a similar point in a letter to Ramsay MacDonald on 12 July 1907,

> We are working very hard and I should like to gently hint that if at any time, you have any spare literature, leaflets, etc., which we are at present too poor to buy, kindly forward them as I want to distribute them amongst the miners who are the last to see daylight and whose thick skulls we must of necessity penetrate because they hold the key of this division (Labour Party Archives, Letter to JR MacDonald).

In his frustrations with the miners, Barker was failing to appreciate the changes taking place. In 1906 and 1908, miners in the YMA had voted to affiliate to the Labour Party. This was against a background of individual miners who were ILP members operating through local YMA branches and influencing the rank and file miners (Taylor, 1992). Political changes were afoot and once the miners switched their votes they became the most loyal and reliable supporters of the Labour Party. In the 1931 debacle the overwhelming majority of seats which Labour managed to hold, were mining constituencies.

In 1918, New Mill and Holmfirth became part of the Colne Valley Constituency. Immediately they were thrown into a General Election in December of that year and one of the foremost COs in the Huddersfield area, Wilfrid Whiteley, was chosen as the Parliamentary candidate. John Beaumont was permitted to leave the Wakefield Work Centre and threw all his energies into the campaign to get a fellow CO elected as the MP.

That election was the first of many Parliamentary contests in which Ernest Beevers was involved. Being a miner and thus in a reserved occupation he did not serve in the armed forces and this gave him greater freedom to campaign in support of Wilfrid Whiteley. If he had been a CO, it could have been an issue with some individuals,

> He had it thrown at him a lot you see but there was a lot of broad-minded people...I remember going and I brought ex-servicemen

down to New Mill Drill Hall from the Mission to listen to Wilfrid Whiteley make his final speech in Holmfirth, a crowded Drill Hall, absolutely packed. There was nearly a rumpus, nearly a fight in that hall. We calmed it down some. We didn't get home while quarter to eleven, walked home and my mother was waiting for us.

Elsewhere in the constituency Whiteley had a more difficult meeting in Saddleworth where one of his election meetings was broken up by soldiers from a local military hospital.

Wilfrid Whiteley was a well-known socialist activist from Huddersfield and had spoken at many meetings throughout the district in the previous two decades. He was a popular figure and his anti-war views were widely known. He had applied to the local tribunal to be a CO but his employer insisted that his work was of national importance and thus his CO status was never formally put to the test. But there wasn't any doubt about his views.

His performance in the election was excellent, bearing in mind he had only one opponent holding the 'Coupon' which meant he had the support of both the Conservative and Liberal Parties.

F W Mallalieu	(Coalition Liberal)	13541	(58.8%)
W Whiteley	(Labour)	9473	(41.2%)
	Majority		4068

That over 41 per cent of the Colne Valley electorate supported Whiteley in the midst of the post-war victory hysteria was perhaps surprising. Labour had never achieved such a high percentage and did not do so again for another three elections. It does support the views of Gladstone Mathers and John Beaumont that the people in the valleys surrounding Huddersfield were quite understanding of those who had held anti-war views.

The local party activists were pleased with the result that they speedily re-selected Whiteley to fight the next General Election. In 1921 however, he was appointed as the secretary/agent to the Huddersfield Labour Party and it was felt he couldn't do both jobs and thus resigned as prospective Parliamentary candidate.

Meanwhile Philip Snowden, who had also been anti-war and had lost the Blackburn seat he had held for twelve years in 1918, showed an interest in Colne Valley. He had some support in the valleys as he was one of the few ILP leaders who had campaigned for Grayson in 1907 and had paid a number of visits to the constituency in the intervening years. His anti-war stance also had earned him respect amongst many ILP members and many remembered his bravery in January 1917 when a group of men from Royal Flying Corps attempted to break-up one of his meetings at the Victoria Hall, Huddersfield (*The Worker*, 3 Feb 1917).

Another factor in his favour was that he was from the Yorkshire Pennines albeit a little further north at Cowling near Keighley. He was particularly good at resonating with the non-conformists in the Constituency and was a really effective orator with his 'come to Jesus' style. Thus it wasn't a surprise that he was selected as Parliamentary candidate in October 1921.

It was clear that another General Election was not too far off and Snowden threw himself into an energetic campaigning regime almost immediately with John Beaumont and the other New Mill Labour members being actively involved in this work. When the election came in November 1922, their efforts were rewarded when Snowden was elected as the MP for Colne Valley.

Snowden was an assiduous MP and a constant campaigner. He'd had an accident when younger which left him disabled but he didn't allow that to hinder his efforts. He won over the doubters in the Labour Party and gained support amongst the voters. There were four general elections in the 1920s and at each one he increased his vote and majority. In 1929 his majority had increased to 9136 and he attracted almost half the votes cast.

In 1924, when Labour formed its first government he was appointed the Chancellor of the Exchequer, a post to which he was re-appointed in 1929. To have an MP holding such a prestigious position in the cabinet was attractive to the voters in the constituency. But of course, it carried with it great responsibility and in 1931, Snowden joined Ramsay MacDonald in forming the National Government with the result that he was expelled from the Labour Party.

Whilst the overwhelming majority of Labour supporters in the constituency disapproved of Snowden's actions in 1931, many still retained a residual affection for him. Both Ernest Beever and John Beaumont were two such people, almost always referring to him as Philip.

John made it clear,

> I knew Philip, although he never came in here - well you see he was
> so lame. It'd be difficult for him getting out of his motor but he
> was a cool logical man.

He completely disagreed however with his actions,

> He went wrong. There were three or four of them - the coalition
> you know. I remember Philip Snowden, I think when there was a
> lot of unemployment and they wanted about a million (£ pounds).
> That were all to help pay unemployment. He said they couldn't
> afford it. Then a while after when the war broke out and they were
> spending many millions a day - and yet they couldn't afford this
> million for the unemployed.

Ernest Beever had an interesting anecdote about Snowden,

> Philip. Oh he used to stay with a pal of mine, John Dearnley up at
> Wooldale...First when he came and at elections he stayed at John's.
> His last election he had in Colne Valley, he told John, he says, 'I'm
> staying at the George Hotel this time'. John says, 'you're going to
> leave the Labour Party. ...Thy'll leave the Labour Party'.

Although Snowden was to triumph at the General Election of 1929, it
did all end in tears and Dearnley's was a truly prophetic statement about
what was to happen two years later.

Whilst Philip Snowden was winning Parliamentary Elections in Colne
Valley, John Beaumont was beginning his career as a local councillor on
New Mill Urban District Council. In April 1925, he was invited to contest the Hepworth seat on the council and, listing his occupation as a
poultry farmer, won comfortably, gaining 92 votes out of 110 cast. But
it wasn't always that easy.

> Then I was up again and I got on the second time by a narrow

squeak. There weren't so many, three put me up... Last three elections, I was on the polls, no bother.

When the council was abolished in 1938, he finished as a councillor and did not contest elections to the new body, Holmfirth UDC. As he explained,

> I gave up. You see my old mother were living, she slept in a room, there at the back of that piano. I'd a shop underneath. It's been taken across the road you see. I'd nearly 300 poultry and a big garden and I was on the council down yonder. I had my hands full I can tell you. Then when they went to Holmfirth, I told them I weren't going. No.

For most of the 1920s and 1930s, John had been a very active councillor and because he had his own small businesses, he was not dependent on any understanding employer. That is what he had planned and it proved to have been the right course of action for him.

After he ceased to be a councillor he continued with his activities in the Labour Party right through to the 1970s. His lifestyle was such that he had time to devote to the Party and also to enjoy reading his beloved books. He was always a thoughtful man and widely respected in the village. John Beaumont was one of those individuals who were held in high esteem and such individuals were essential to the establishment and development of the Labour Party in villages such as Hepworth.

He died, aged 91 on 22 August 1979.

Quotations of James Beaumont from interview with David Clark on 22 November 1974, of Joe Driver on 18 November 1974, of Ernest Beever on 15 November 1974 and of Edna Mosley on 26 May 1976.

7

Connie Lewcock
1894-1980

To my eyes, one of the most beautiful buildings in the world is Durham Cathedral, standing as it does proud and magnificent on its rocky promontory above the River Wear. It was founded in 1093 and is widely regarded as one of the finest examples of Norman architecture.

As I travelled on my weekly journey to and from Westminster, for almost a quarter of a century as the MP for South Shields, this was vision which greeted me, at its best from the railway train as it passed through Durham Station. As I sat in awe at its splendour, I was forever reminded that it could have once been destroyed in the early decades of the twentieth-century, by a later doyenne of North East Labour politics, Connie Lewcock OBE. Thankfully, at the last moment she had second thoughts about dynamiting what is now deemed a World Heritage Site. The Cathedral still stands in all its glory presiding over the ancient city where miners continue to pay their annual homage within its walls on the day of the 'Big Meeting'.

In later years, Connie Lewcock became part of Newcastle's Labour establishment but she was not from the North East. She was born Constance Mary (Connie) on 11 April 1894 in the small market town of Horncastle in Lincolnshire, being the only daughter of Thomas H Ellis, who owned a draper's shop, and his wife Emily Mary. She however, did not know her father for long, for he died when she was only four, which had a devastating effect on her. She was from an early age, a strong-willed girl with firm opinions, doubtless fuelled by her avid reading habits. She simply loved books.

Matters did not get easier when her mother married again to the local Methodist minister, whom the young Connie detested, regarding her mother's action as a betrayal of her father. The couple moved to Slough but it was decided that Connie would remain in Horncastle with her aunt who also ran a shop there. She had already showed signs of developing a rebellious streak but she now added loneliness and a certain wilfulness. She set out to shock the people of her small home town and even began smoking in public.

However, with her love of literature, she excelled at school and won a scholarship to the town's Queen Elizabeth's Grammar School where she entertained ambitions to read for a university degree which was itself unusual for a woman in the early twentieth-century. She matriculated from the University of London but eventually, much to her disappointment, was unsuccessful at the inter-stage of a BA degree in Arts.

Connie Lewcock campaigning as a suffragette c.1912-14

But in truth she might have been side-tracked away from academic studies by her other varied interests. In 1908, she had become deeply committed to the suffrage cause. Whilst on a holiday to the Scottish resort of Dunoon with her mother and stepfather, she had heard a suffragette speaking on the promenade and become completely captivated. As she was later to explain,

> I saw a woman talking about freedom and equality and it changed the whole of my life at fourteen. I don't know who she was but it was like St Paul at Damascus. It changed the whole of my life. I went back to Lincolnshire and applied to be in the Women's Social and Political Union (WSPU) and they said that I was fourteen and not eligible for membership, but they would make an exception for me and they made an exception. I started giving out handbills demanding the vote and they crumpled them up and tossed them in the gutter. So I decided that there was nothing in it for me.

Eventually, in 1911, when it had become clear she wasn't going to be accepted by the University of London, she found a job at £50 a year as an uncertified teacher in the mining village of Esh Winning, five miles to the west of Durham City. She had a somewhat challenging introduction to the school,

> It was a pit village and there were seventy-eight boys and girls in standard four. I was taken by the headmaster to get the class and he said to me, 'Have you got a cane?' I said, 'No, I didn't know I should need a cane,' and he said, 'well you will'. I had a breakdown on three months and after that I went home

Connie was a resilient character and made a speedy recovery before returning north. The Durham Coalfield was a marked contrast to the rural agricultural district of Lincolnshire where she had grown up, but once she overcame the initial shock, she adapted comfortably to her new environment. As a lively, seventeen year old, she quickly began to make friends in the local community, especially amongst the younger miners.

In her spare time she became a familiar figure as she cycled around the district delivering leaflets and holding open-air meetings outlining the suffragette case. She claimed she did not meet a great deal of resistance but on the contrary found considerable support amongst the local branches of the ILP. This was especially so in the Cornsay Branch which encompassed the surrounding villages including Esh Winning. It was fortunate for Connie that the secretary of the Cornsay ILP was John Harrison who was a keen supporter of 'Votes for Women'. His mother Elizabeth was an active member of the WPSU and held meetings in her house. Later John was to marry Isabella Faulkner, another committed member of the WPSU. Isabella was from a mining family and became a teacher in nearby Chester le Street. She accompanied Connie and John's sister, Esther Harrison, to public meetings and in distributing campaign literature. Thus, there was active support for the WPSU rooted in the working class community and this in turn had direct links into the local ILP (Jones, 2013 pp. 86-103).

The ILP, of all the political parties, was the most supportive of the suffrage movement and Connie began to build relationships with ILP members throughout County Durham which would grow even closer as the years passed and especially so, following the declaration of war in 1914. Connie's experiences were paralleled with many other young suffragette supporters who were often attracted to politics initially on the single subject issue, 'Votes for Women', but then began to consider the wider political system. Many became lifelong activists in the ILP and later, the Labour Party.

Connie's life outside school was dominated by this increasing interest in politics. The suffragette cause was still the driving force of her activities but she was a member of the ILP by early 1913 and this was taking up an increasing amount of her time. Furthermore as part of her suffragette campaigning she attended public meetings of the two traditional parties to put the women's case. Usually, she had a poor reception and was manhandled by the stewards as they evicted her from the meetings.

This eventually led to a firm friendship developing with a young miner from Quebec pit who was also an active member of the local ILP,

> I had a friend, a pitman who was called Joss Craddock. He came to me and said, 'Have you bruised yourself?' I said it was the stewards chucked me out at the meeting and he said, 'I didn't believe you when you told me'.
>
> Then he said, 'I'll come with you next time' and so I said, 'Well, I'm going on Friday to a Liberal meeting and I'll take you with me'. He sat five seats in front of me in the balcony and I got up and asked my question and the stewards moved to chuck me out. There

was calm going on. It was unusual for there to be calm. The stewards usually chucked you down on the floor and they put you out. This was what Joss wanted, he squared up to them, the stewards, and said, 'Go on lass. I can keep them here all night' and so I had about a five minute speech from the balcony. The stewards tapped me on the shoulder and they said, 'Madam, if you and your friend would like to go out without any disturbance, it will be alright with us'. So we walked out with the honours of war.

There was an active group of suffragettes in the North East and Connie was determined to make her presence felt within it,

I went to the Blackett Street office of the WPSU on the Saturday and said, 'I can do anything you want me to do', and they said, 'Well you're not to get arrested because Mrs Pankhurst has laid it down that only people over twenty-one will be arrested'.

That was in 1912. She followed her leader's edict and in spite of extremely energetic campaigning involving breaches of the law, she managed to avoid arrest. She quickly became widely known in the North East suffragette circles and knew the leaders including Emily Davison who was killed on 4 June 1913, when she fell under the King's horse at Epsom, the only suffragette who died for the cause.

I knew her and was at her funeral. But men used to say, men have died for the vote, why don't women die for the vote and I think that it was necessary to die for the vote. I've never considered it but I think I would now.

Connie Ellis was very moved by Emily Davison's sacrifice and felt it incumbent on others such as herself to step up the militant campaigning. In the North East there was a great deal of activity which largely took the form of fire-raising in which Connie played her part. She set fire to Durham City railway station but not with a great deal of success. However she achieved much more with her next initiative, the burning down of Esh Winning railway station. This was accomplished with the assistance of her new found friend, the young miner, Josh Craddock.

I was in confidence with Joss and Emily Davison died and I thought something had to be done and I said to Joss if you'll burn down the station, I'll leave the clues. He left a handkerchief with a 'C' on it and some brown hairpins. It was a very trifling affair but it got into the papers and the policeman came down to the school in the morning and the headmaster said he'd never had a policeman come to interview a teacher before. He said, 'Is this your handkerchief?' And I said, 'Yes, I can identify it but there are many thousands of handkerchiefs with 'C' on'. He said, 'Can you identify these brown hairpins?' and I said, 'No. I can't identify them'.

Connie was very proud of this incident, describing it as 'the perfect crime'. Having instructed the loyal Joss to set the building on fire, she had attended a public meeting a few miles away and thus could produce a number of independent witnesses. Although the authorities had their suspicions they were unable to prove anything.

The headmaster went to the school and he said that he'd had a heart attack over me. I was called up in June 1914 to give an undertaking that I wouldn't do any political meetings and I said I wouldn't (give the undertaking). So they gave me a month's notice and I went home thinking that my teaching career was over. The territorials were called up in July and August 1914 and I got a telegram asking me to go to Brandon School which had the worst headmaster in the county. He took a fancy to me, he called me 'ginger', which I was then. He said what did I want there, and I was knocking my knees together. I was frightened and I said 'I've come to work' and he said, 'Well that's a damn good job because nobody else does'.

When this supply teacher asked whether I'd be given my notice he said, 'I like her. She'll be teaching here'. So I taught there until I found it unbearable. He was a very patriotic person and I objected to the First World War.

Connie's political activities continued apace. They were dominating her life and she found it exhilarating and exciting. Until the outbreak of the war, she continued to be very active in the suffragette cause but then she became disillusioned by such leaders as Emmeline Pankhurst who was enthusiastically pro-war. Given her own opposition to the hostilities, not surprisingly she disagreed with the official policy to suspend the suffrage campaign during the war. She gradually switched most of her energies to the ILP where she found many kindred spirits who shared her views on the war.

Before war was declared however, she still felt the need to keep the suffrage profile high by means of publicity stunts which were aimed at shocking the public. So she decided to 'go for the big one' and blow up the iconic Durham Cathedral. Since arriving in Esh Winning in 1911, she had built close contacts with the ILP branches and the many younger miners who were members. A considerable amount of planning went into this dramatic plan, the building was studied and the best location identified where the bomb should be placed as well as the amount of explosives necessary.

Connie succinctly explained some background,

> I had a friend Will Lawther, who was to become President of the Mineworkers Federation of Great Britain, (later the National Union of Mineworkers). He was at Chopwell in the meantime and he was an anarchist when I met him. He offered to get me some explosives to do the necessary. I considered it and I thought that it would not be a good idea because I'd blow myself up.

Connie may have dismissed the proposal in a rather cursory fashion but she did explain to me that they had invested a great deal of effort in trying to see if the Cathedral could be blown up. She had access to individuals who were familiar with using explosives in the pits and understood the best places to effect damage. In answer to a question if she would have gone through with the plan, 'If you thought you could have got yourself out'. She replied simply, 'Yes'. On reflection after sixty years, she had the good grace to admit, 'I'm thankful that I didn't do it now'.

Will Lawther was a member of an extensive political family in the pit village of Chopwell, which was commonly referred to as 'Little Moscow'. The village was a stronghold of the Labour and Communist Parties. It is famous for still having streets named after Hardie, Engels, Lenin and Marx. The local miners' banner had depicted their Labour MP elected in

1906, John W Taylor, but this was replaced in 1907 by one featuring the portraits of the Labour Party leader, Keir Hardie, with Lenin and Karl Marx. Will was born across the Tyne in Choppington, Northumberland and developed his political views in this left-wing environment and was regarded very much as firebrand in his early years. Soon after moving to Chopwell in the early 1900s, he became secretary of the local ILP branch.

He became active in both the Durham Miners' Association and the Labour Party and was selected as the Labour Parliamentary Candidate for South Shields in the General Elections of 1922, 1923 and 1924. Although unsuccessful, he increased the Labour share of the vote but never came closer to winning than in 1922 when he failed by a mere 25 votes. In 1929 however, he was elected as MP for Bishop Auckland which he was to lose two years later (Clark, 1992 pp.56-61).

A South Shields councillor of the time and fellow miner, Bill Blyton, later MP for neighbouring Houghton le Spring and a Labour Peer, always maintained that Will in those days was seen as too extreme and failed to persuade sufficient of the many Liberal working class voters to switch to Labour. It was left to the more mainstream, Chuter Ede, to do that and to win the seat and make it one of Labour's strongholds. Indeed South Shields is the only constituency in Great Britain which has had its own MP since 1832 and never yet returned a Conservative.

Connie Ellis had reasons other than politics to remain in County Durham when war was declared. As her interest in socialism increased, she began attending a Socialist Sunday School in Chopwell with life-changing repercussions,

> I went to Chopwell, Sunday May 1st and I saw a young man look-ing at me. I didn't speak to him but I went home and told my land-lady, 'I've seen the man I'm going to marry', and she said, 'What's his name?' I said, 'I don't know his name but we shall meet again', and he went home and said the same thing.

The young man in question was William Best Lewcock (Will), a miner from Westerhope on the edge of Newcastle and a fellow member of the ILP. Because it was May Day, he had travelled to Chopwell to celebrate socialism's international day at the Socialist Sunday School. They did meet again and the relationship developed and blossomed. After four years of courtship under difficult conditions, they eventually married at Horncastle Congregational Church on 6 August 1918, notwithstanding many happenings to both of them along the way.

During World War I, Will encountered problems at work from an unexpected quarter, his workmates. He had been absent from the pit for a period after winning a trade union scholarship to Ruskin College, Oxford and whilst there, declared himself to be a conscientious objector. As his fiancée explained,

> The pitmen held a meeting and said that they wouldn't work with him. He went to the lodge meeting and he said 'I've always been on your side men, and I won't be against you now. I'll leave'. He resigned immediately but ironically he didn't need to be a conscientious objector because he was in a protected occupation.

Whilst many active members of the ILP were opposed to the war, most members of the Labour Party followed the patriotic line, including many miners. Indeed, my own grandfather, Isaac Smith, who was a miner in the Durham Coalfield and later a Labour councillor, volunteered for the army at the age of 39. He was a married man with four children and enlisted into the Yorkshire and Lancashire Regiment. He served on the Western Front digging tunnels under enemy lines.

Furthermore, there were also some on the left of the Labour Party such as Robert Blatchford and Victor Grayson who supported the war, the latter fought in the trenches. Even members of the ILP were divided on the issue. In a survey in Bradford by the ILP branch in February 1916, prior to conscription becoming effective, it was found that,

> A census in February 1916 indicated that of 461 young men in the local Party membership of 1473, 113 were in the trenches…118 were in training in England, 6 were in the navy and 207 were attested under the Derby Scheme as necessary home workers. A similar survey in 1918 found that of 492 members liable for service, 351 were serving in the forces whilst 48 were conscientious objectors or on national work (Jowitt and Laybourn, 1992 p.170).

Having lost his job as a miner and with it the status of a protected occupation, Will had to find other statutory protected employment which he did in agriculture, tending tomatoes for Charles Coates on Teesside. Coates was a successful exporter from Middlesbrough and chairman of Cleveland ILP was thus sympathetic to Will's predicament.

Meanwhile in 1916, Connie ceased teaching at Brandon and managed to obtain work in a political capacity with the National Federation of Women Workers (NFWW). It all happened in an unexpected way as Connie explained,

> The thing was to get women into the ammunition factories and I wouldn't have any part of that. I went into Newcastle on the Saturday and I went to the National Federation of Women Workers who were holding a meeting on the Sunday afternoon and they asked me to speak. They couldn't get this speaker who was scheduled and they asked me. I addressed a meeting in the Pavilion in Newcastle and I was scared of two thousand women. I was not scared of open air meetings but scared of an indoor meeting. They asked me to go and train for the Women Workers. I went down to London for six weeks and was put in Middlesbrough.
>
> I went to the Dorman Long's factory which they were beginning to organise. I sat under a railway train carriage with four or five women and we started the union. It was snowing. I had concern about the lead workers. They were grinding paint and I went to them and I organised them. There were only about eight of them and I said now you can have lemon and milk drinks and if necessary, face masks. They said we'll get the sack and I said well you'll die of lead poisoning if you don't. They said they'd rather die of lead poisoning than from getting the sack and they went out of the union.
>
> I was going to a firm in Stockton, I don't remember the name, and there's a policeman at the door. He said if I think you've seen a trade union woman here and I said, 'No. I haven't.' Because I didn't see myself. He said, 'I'm stationed here to prevent a meeting and if you go down this lane and went on until you come to a gate, the women come out there as soon as the lunch bell goes'. I swear he winked at me. I went down the lane and organised them. I got

up on a chair and addressed them and they made horns for mines.

I went to Greatham's, which was the salt company (Cerebos was the actual name of the company) then and I stood on the fence and they grabbed my ankles, people grabbed my ankles so that I shouldn't fall off and I got a thousand of them.

Connie worked with the NFWW in Middlesbrough for a little over a year and gained useful experience as an organiser. It was very convenient being on Teesside, as Will was also living there. Connie felt a little aggrieved about her weekly pay maintaining that it was a bit incongruous that she making claims at tribunals for wages of £3 a week when she herself was only being paid £2. As it happened, it was through Will that she got to know Charles Coates, his employer and who largely financed the Cleveland ILP. In 1917, a vacancy arose for an organiser for the Cleveland ILP and Connie successfully applied. 'I was friendly with the chairman of Cleveland ILP and his wife who was in the Freedom League, the Women's Freedom League and I think I didn't have a chance of not getting it'.

The Women's Freedom League (WFL) was a suffrage organisation and was formed as a breakaway from the WSPU by individuals who objected to Emmeline and Christabel Pankhursts' decision to abandon the annual conference and to run the WPSU by a committee. The founders of the breakaway body objected to the Pankhursts' highhanded attitude and their rejection of democracy within the WSPU.

The Coates' were a prosperous local family and the three children, Charles, Walter and Marion all became prominent in the local ILP. The two brothers became close friends of the well-known American industrialist and social reformer, Joseph Fels, and in the 1890s Marion travelled to the USA to work as a nanny in his household in Philadelphia. On her return to England she became deeply involved in the WPSU until she fell out with the Pankhursts and helped form the WFL. In the early 1900s, she married Frederick Hansen from another well-to-do Middlesbrough family who were involved in the socialist cause. Marion became secretary of the local ILP and after World War I she was elected to Middlesbrough Borough Council. In 1910, Charles married another formidable woman, Alice, whom he rescued from attack whilst she was addressing an open-air meeting. She too was active in the WSPU and WFL, spending a short time in prison for her suffragist activities. In 1919 she was the first woman to be elected to the local council and remained active in public life until the late 1950s.

The Coates family largely financed the ILP locally and Connie's weekly wage was £5 which was relatively generous, compared with the £2 a week with the NFWW and a mere £50 a year as an unqualified teacher. Connie was a little ungracious to her benefactors, explaining their actions in a rather cavalier fashion, 'he was rich and it bothered him to be rich out of exporting coal to Norway'.

As the organiser she covered a large area, stretching from the industrial areas of Stockton and Middlesbrough in the north, across the North Yorkshire Moors to the fishing town of Whitby and down to the seaside resort of Scarborough. Such was the comradeship of the ILP in the area, Connie maintained that during the two years she was organiser she never once stayed in a hotel, always finding accommodation with party members. Her job was to arrange speakers to visit communities, putting the socialist case and often speaking herself. She listed a galaxy of propagandists including Walton Newbold, Sylvia Pankhurst, Manny Shinwell and the ubiquitous, Katherine Bruce Glasier whom she admitted she especially 'liked'.

Connie had only one serious run-in with the law when she was arrested and sentenced,

> I remember being summoned to Guisborough to make my defence to a charge of making inflammatory speeches. But I was careful to say that the capitalist didn't care whether he supplied bad meat or good meat to the soldiers in the trenches. It was a case of profit and I didn't say that they supplied bad meat. They got a witness against me who said that I'd said that they supplied bad meat to the soldiers.

She was found guilty and fined £5 which to her chagrin the Cleveland ILP paid on her behalf. Later she claimed she had been framed. Apparently some years later, when she was in Loftus further down the coast,

> A man came to me and said, 'Are you Connie Ellis,' and I said, 'Yes,

I'm Connie Lewcock now but I was Connie Ellis'. He said, 'I want to tell you that it was all a pack of lies. I signed the statement and I couldn't go back on it'.

In 1919, after the war controls ceased, Will was released from his obligation to work in agriculture and as it wasn't deemed acceptable for him to return to the pit, he applied for a job as the Labour organiser in Stroud, which was financed by the Union of Post Office Workers. Rural Gloucestershire was a far cry from the industrial North East and Connie found it, '...very beautiful…it was difficult to say how it was different but there were small firms that made chairs and bedsteads'.

They were very happy with every intention of settling there and bought a house for £320 but their joys were short-lived for the union discovered some discrepancies in their candidate's accounts and in 1921 they were required to move to Newport in Monmouthshire. The candidate there was J W 'Bill' Bowen who fought the seat at five elections to no avail although he did provide focus and stability which assisted Connie and Will to successfully develop the party organization in the constituency.

Throughout all these years, Connie remained without full-time employment but helped Will in his work, speaking at meetings and generally assisting him. They both loved the work and were extremely effective at it. The 1920s were tumultuous years for Labour as the party sought to establish itself as the Official Opposition Party and on two occasions actually formed the government. Inevitably this led to strains in the movement notably between the ILP and the growing Labour Party.

Newport was no exception as Connie explained,

> We had a quarrel with the ILP in Newport in 1920 and 1923. We (the Labour Party) wanted to do propaganda and the ILP suggested that it was essential for them to do the propaganda and we quarreled about it. Arthur Henderson came down and asked us to state our case. We stated it and he brought his hand down on the table and he said, 'Shut up,' and we shut up. He regarded the quarrel between the ILP and the Labour Party as disastrous which it was and the ILP faded away.

This was a difficult period for many Labour activists as it must be remembered that it wasn't until the Labour Party Constitution of 1918 that individual membership was permitted for the first time and until then, many activists had been members of the ILP. Most of these, including Connie and Will remained in the ILP for a short period out of loyalty before switching their political activities solely to the Labour Party.

The family remained in Newport for eleven years, bought a house there and built up a particularly well-organised Constituency Labour Party (CLP). Newport was somewhat different from the more traditional South Wales parties in that the trade unions were not as much an integral part of the CLP which relied more heavily upon individual membership. One result of this was that it was not as radical and tended to remain loyal to the national leadership. Much of this success in the constituency was due to the efforts of Will and Connie Lewcock.

Newport was traditionally a Liberal seat although with a strong Conservative vote even amongst some sectors of the working-class. Labour had contested the constituency in 1906 but attracted only 16.5 per cent of the vote and then didn't contest the two following General Elections of 1910. In 1918, it entered the fray yet again, increasing its share of the poll dramatically to 41 per cent. Then in spite of the best efforts of the Lewcocks and a growing local party, success eluded it in the by-election of 1922, when it polled 33.8 per cent.

The party was similarly unsuccessful in the General Elections of 1922 attracting 45.7 per cent of the vote and in a three-cornered contest in 1923, its share fell to 38.6 per cent of the votes cast. In 1924 however, in a straight fight, the share increased to a high of 47.2 per cent. In 1929, victory final came with James Young gaining the seat which he was unable to hold in 1931 although polling a very credible 40.9 per cent. The Party then had to wait until 1945 before the seat was regained and it became a safe Labour seat.

These rather disappointing Parliamentary election results masked the massive effort of the local party activists. Although unable to rely on the support they might have expected from the local trade union branches, Will and Connie, spent a vast amount of effort in building up the party. It had the highest number of individual members of any Welsh constituency and the fourth highest in Great Britain with these figures including an exceptionally high number of women. The national party leadership was keen that areas such as Newport should root the local party within the community and the Lewcocks responded with enthusiasm. Connie was elected to the local council and the central party leadership often cited Newport as amongst its best exemplars (*Labour Organiser* 1930-4).

The women members' role was not confined to 'making the tea', as the surviving minutes of the party repeatedly record women raising issues which were of particular interest to other women such as birth control, family allowances, raising of the school leaving age and housing. Furthermore the CLP sent two delegates each year to the national conference, one of whom was a woman.

The key to this involvement in the community and also to the party's finance was the extent of the social activity which tended to be organised by the women. There were the usual activities such as raffles and also larger draws on specific occasions such as Christmas or the Derby. By 1927, the party minutes record that women ensured that every ward held regular dances and socials at the local Labour halls with between ten to twenty percent of the CLPs income regularly coming from these sources. In 1928, the local Labour Party remarkably provided for three thousand children to have an outing. By such means, Labour became deeply rooted in the communities of Newport which ultimately provided the continuing political base for the CLP (Tanner, nd).

The instigation for this activity came from Connie and Will. They recognised how essential the strategy was and worked indefatigably for its success. The leadership of the Party nationally recognised this and in 1932, when a vacancy arose for an organiser in the North of England, Will decided he would like to return North and successfully applied.

The appointment was to cover the Northern Region and Yorkshire working alongside Margaret Gibb. Connie recalled, 'I wanted to live in York and I said to my husband, "Buy a house in York if you can. They'll want us to live in Leeds".' Fortunately York was a busy railway hub and from there, Will could conveniently travel all over Yorkshire and the North East. Meanwhile, with her children growing up Connie often accompanied him especially enjoying by-elections such as the one in Colne Valley in 1939.

In 1942 the boundaries of the Party's region structure changed with most of Yorkshire being detached from the North East whilst

Cumberland was added to form a Northern Region. This gave Will the opportunity to return to live in his native Northeast and Connie was pleased to be returning to her adopted region. They bought a house in Pelton, a small village in County Durham near Chester le Street and Will travelled into Newcastle to the office. Connie describes her thoughts at the time when the prospects of victory seemed far removed,

> I wanted to fight Hitler and I moved to a smallholding near Pelton. I was over call-up age and Peter was flat-footed and he couldn't march. He would have been peeling potatoes all the war and so he wanted to experience agricultural work. We got worried about Hitler and Mussolini. I knew I was on the list for Hitler, that Will would be and our children (Sheila, Peter and Cynthia) would be, so I sent Cynthia to Canada.

During her years of work for the Party, Connie met many of the Labour leaders and held strong opinions about them. Ramsay MacDonald she admired in his early years and especially when holding onto his principles in opposing World War I, describing him as a 'marvellous speaker'. But like most Labour Party members, she changed her views completely after his defection in 1931,

> We thought that he was a traitor. Well he was going down on the train with Josh Ritson, the MP for Durham, and he was talking about Lady Londonderry. She was spiritual and she was, oh marvellous and she was wonderful. And Josh Ritson said, 'I thought the bugger was daft'.

Her views on Philip Snowden were similar, he too was a 'good speaker'. However, she reserved the accolade of the best speaker for Emmeline Pankhurst, although before World War I she had already lost all faith in her although retaining her admiration for her daughter, Sylvia.

Will continued to work as regional organiser alongside the redoubtable Margaret Gibb until 1955 and they proved a formidable team. In the late 1940s, the Lewcocks moved to West Denton within the Newcastle City boundaries and in 1956, following his retirement, he was elected to the City Council and served until his death in 1960.

Then Connie succeeded him on the City Council for the Benwell Ward, serving with great distinction and passion until 1971. She held a number of senior posts including, Chair of the Housing Management Committee, the Parliamentary and General Purposes Committee as well as being Vice-chair of the powerful Finance Committee. In his valedictory comments, the Leader of Newcastle City Council, Jeremy Beecham, later a Labour Peer, described her as a remarkable character who was an inspiration to the Labour movement and who brought a humanising effect to local government.

Connie Lewcock recalling her suffragette years in the 1970s

On a cold winter's day in 1980 she slipped and fell outside her house in West Denton where she had lived for over thirty years and died on 11 November 1980 just up the road in Newcastle General Hospital.

She was proud to have been awarded an OBE in 1966 for her lifetime of public service. In a sense, much of that public service was alongside her husband Will. Wherever they worked for the Labour Party, they did so as a team. Indeed when her marriage was approaching in 1918, a friend had counselled her, 'If you marry Will, you'll always be second to the Cause'. To which Connie replied immediately, 'I should hope so'.

Quotations of Connie Lewcock from interviews with David Clark on 12 February 1979 and 22 March 1979.

8

Margaret Gibb
1892-1984

Twenty or so miles from Tyneside, lies the magnificent stately home of Wallington. On the surface it appears a traditional National Trust property but it contains unusual secrets. In 1942, during the darkest days of World War Two, the owner, Sir Charles Trevelyan, a former Labour MP for Newcastle Central and Cabinet Minister, gifted it to the nation. I always took a perverse pleasure in viewing photographs of the Labour Cabinets of the 1920s hanging on the walls of the its fine rooms.

There were to be more surprises to be found in the adjoining buildings now used by the visitors to this grand house. Sir Charles and his family never sought to hide their political allegiance and were always supportive of projects which helped the Labour Party. They worked closely with the Regional Office and in particular with a young, energetic, regional officer, Margaret Gibb, who from 1930 was responsible for building up Labour's strength especially amongst the women of the region. She organised meetings, sports and other activities in the grounds of the house and in the outbuildings today are large photographs of Labour Party activists in the 1930s having picnics and meetings on the manicured lawns. A far cry from the environment in which most of the participants lived and worked!

A mile or so to the north in the estate village of Cambo, Margaret Gibb lived with her lifelong friend, Molly Thompson. Margaret had moved into the cottage, The Riding, which was part of the integrated village complex in 1951 and lived there until her death at the age of ninety-one in 1984. It was always a pleasure to visit the delightful terraced cottage to talk with this remarkable woman. Although, well into her eighties when

I knew her best, she had a clear mind and vivid recollections of experiences from her long career serving the Labour Party until her retirement in 1957. She was a tall, handsome woman who spoke in a concise and straightforward manner, which perhaps was a reflection of her training as a teacher. From her years of public speaking, as well as dealing with volunteers in her work, she knew how to use her voice to considerable effect and would slip into a softer version of her childhood Tyneside lilt when it suited her.

Margaret Hunter Harrison was born on 31 July 1892 into a middle class family. Her father was a commercial traveller for a timber company but Margaret had no recollection of him as he died in December 1893, only 18 months after her birth. However if she could claim any political antecedents it was from her father. He was a radical Liberal - much too much so for the official party - and heavily committed to campaigning for progressive causes. Indeed, later when her mother was questioning her commitment to Labour and the ILP, Margaret would retort that had her father still been alive, he would have been a committed socialist.

Margaret was brought up in an all-female household, for following her father's death, her mother moved in with her own mother and a maiden aunt, who was a schoolteacher. This was in Dunston which was situated on the banks of the River Tyne between Gateshead and Blaydon. Margaret was one of the early beneficiaries of the Education Act of 1902 which greatly enhanced the opportunities for secondary education. In 1906, she passed the examinations to attend Blaydon Secondary School where she spent four happy years. In 1910, she decided to train as teacher and went to St Hilda's Training College in Durham for two years, where a negative approach disappointed her,

> My secondary school, in spite of all its limitations, it was just four rooms over the council chamber, but that school meant far more to me than ever the training college did. The training college attitude was to do as you're told and there were restrictions everywhere. Now in secondary school we'd been encouraged to take our own decisions up to a point even in those days. But there was nothing of that in college. Of course it was a Church of England college but I think they were all very much alike at that time.

On leaving college she found a position teaching in a mixed school at Crookhill, a few miles from her home. This was a working class community on the northern edge of the Durham Coalfield thus she was teaching the children of miners and other industrial workers. During World War I, with many male teachers being recruited into the army, she was transferred to a boys' school in Blaydon for the remainder of the hostilities. When the war ended, she returned to the school at Crookhill until 1923 when she married and had to resign as Durham County Council, like most educational authorities, did not employ married women as teachers.

From an early age, Margaret appears to have been interested in events around her. She recalls going to meetings during the 1906 General Election when she was only 14. Although the election was in January, some of the meetings, especially Labour's, would have been held out of doors. Dunston, where she lived, was in Chester le Street Constituency which in 1906 had a particularly interesting contest. Although the majority of voters in the division were miners, they had generally supported a mine owner, Sir James Joicey, as the Liberal MP. By 1906 however, many had become disenchanted and switched their support to John Wilkinson Taylor who was a member of the ILP and General Secretary of the Durham Miners' Mechanics Association. He won the seat easily and continued as MP until he retired on grounds of ill health in 1919. In 1906 he stood as an independent Labour candidate and on arriving at Westminster immediately joined the Labour Group of MPs, beginning a remarkable record of over a hundred years of continuous Labour representation in the constituency.

It was in the course of the election of January 1910 that Margaret recalled seeing the Labour Leader, Keir Hardie.

> Taylor was our Labour Member and the place for his big meetings in the village was called the Lecture Hall and it belonged to the Methodists. Now they had let the hall for a meeting for Taylor and Keir Hardie. This is all a bit vague to me but I do remember going down onto the Main Street…When the trustees of the Lecture Hall discovered that Keir Hardie was coming to this meeting, they cancelled the booking and the only thing that could be done was either to have the meeting there (in the open-air) or abandon it

altogether. I saw this man, Keir Hardie, talking to quite a considerable crowd.

By the election of December 1910, her interest in politics had grown and she attended a number of political meetings. In this period, Margaret was still following in her father's footsteps and supporting the Liberals. She took the train across the Tyne to Newcastle to hear the Foreign Secretary, Sir Edward Grey and also made the short journey to the adjacent constituency of Gateshead, to support the successful Liberal candidate, Sir Harold Elverston.

World War I politicised Margaret and led eventually to her switching her political allegiance. She was bitterly opposed to the hostilities and followed a pacifist line. A number of the more radical Liberal MPs, such as Sir Charles Trevelyan, who hailed from Northumberland but represented Elland, shared her views on the War, but it was Asquith, a Liberal Prime Minister who took Britain into it and another, Lloyd George who kept the country in. She became increasingly attracted to the ILP whose leaders were united in opposing the war. Her opinions were becoming even more fixed and she caused considerable consternation at school when she refused to celebrate Empire Day. Fortunately a fellow teacher at the school shared her views. Thus, they travelled together to political meetings and anti-war demonstrations and were able to give each other mutual support.

When the General Election of 1918 came in December, she enthusiastically threw herself into Labour's campaign in the newly created Blaydon Constituency where William Whiteley was the candidate. Margaret explained her entry to a lifetime of Labour politics,

> I went to Labour Party meetings then I don't think I did anything. No I did. I went to the agent at the meeting in the Electoral Hall in the village of Dunston and said I didn't know what I could do but if there was anything that I could do. So he told me where to go. Immediately after in 1919, I think there was a Labour Party meeting and Whiteley, who was the Labour candidate came. I joined that night.

That was in the January 1919 and a couple of months later she also joined the local branch of the ILP and was soon elected vice-chairman. Even more significantly, in March of the same year, she saw a poster for the inaugural meeting of a women's section of the Labour Party and went. She described in some detail the meeting, which was to influence her approach to politics for the rest of her long life,

> …There were exactly four of us there, exactly four. Lillian Anderson Fenn was then the organiser and she was a brilliant woman. She talked to us as though we were four thousand and I think we began to think we were four thousand…Within three months we'd over seventy people coming to that meeting.

At the meeting, Margaret was appointed the secretary of the women's section and so began a lifetime of work for Labour. They needed to raise money for their propaganda activities and did so by sales of work, raffles, collections and supper evenings. They were repeatedly helped out by Jack Gilliland, the political agent of the Durham Miners' Association responsible for Blaydon and Chester le Street. He supplied the minute books, headed letters and all the correspondence. Margaret described him being as 'keen as mustard on getting a women's section in every spot he could'.

By 1921, she was extremely active and joined other Labour women from throughout the county as a founder member of the Durham Labour Women's Advisory Council which was to continue for over seventy years. It became an extremely powerful body and was crucial to the development and organisation of women's sections in the county for many decades.

> …I found myself going more and more into extra ILP things, you know. Westfield Hall in Gateshead was the great centre for activity and of course Diana Street in Newcastle. Sir Charles (Trevelyan) bought this hall, a little wooden hall of course, and that was our centre in Newcastle. You just made a bee-line for Diana Street or you made a bee-line for Westfield Hall in Gateshead. A lot of Ruth Dodd's (Gateshead author, business woman and Labour councillor) money was behind Westfield Hall.

It was whilst attending a public speaking class at Westfield Hall that Margaret Harrison met her future husband, Tom Gibb, who was the full-time Labour agent for Jarrow and an organiser for the ILP. They married in 1923.

Being married meant that Margaret had to resign as a teacher at Crookhill School. Tom had moved to be agent in Morpeth but the Constituency Labour Party ran short of funds and he transferred to near-by Blyth. The money ran out there as well and the young couple moved to Hartlepool where Tom's health gave way. Margaret managed to obtain a headship in a village school at Stevington in Bedfordshire, where the County Council took a much more liberal approach to these matters and did employ married women. The couple remained there for three years and Margaret continued with her Labour Party activities, forming a highly successful women's section which met in the school house.

Their stay at Stevington coincided with the General Strike of 1926 and the miners' lockout. Margaret and Tom decided they couldn't sit idly by so,

> In the miners' lockout, we went to the village cross which was in the middle of the village and took a collection for the miners. My husband and I ran the meeting between us and we got a collection considerably over £2. It was getting on for £3 that was a lot of money then (approximately £150 in 2015 values). This was a village of agricultural workers and low paid railway workers and to get £1, never mind getting on for £3, a collection round the cross was very very good because the bulk of them have never seen a miner.

In the more relaxing atmosphere of rural Bedfordshire, Tom's health gradually improved and towards the end of 1926, he went to Sheffield Central to act as the agent for the Prospective Parliamentary Candidate, Philip C Hoffman. Margaret had to serve her notice as headmistress before she joined him three months later. Margaret was excited to get back into the cut and thrust of political life as she explained,

> I got to Sheffield in February 1927 and a very different life from a quiet agricultural village. Not a terribly reactionary village, I'll

admit that, but still a quiet village life and to come to the hurly burly of Sheffield at that time. They'd just taken control of the Council and they used to have to control the people coming into the gallery to listen to the council meetings and they always turned away far more than they could let in. That was the interest in the whole thing.

Unfortunately, Tom's health deteriorated once more and he died at the end of July 1927. Margaret needed a job herself then and received an informal offer as a headmistress from a Durham County councillor. At the same time she was offered the agent's job in Sheffield and, deciding to remain in politics, she accepted and helped Hoffman win the seat at the 1929 General Election. In the same year, she was elected as a councillor for Moor Ward on Sheffield City Council, serving on the Education Committee.

Unexpectedly, towards the end of 1929, one of the Labour Party's agents for the North East of England died and Margaret was chosen for the position out of 127 applicants. She resigned as a Sheffield councillor and early in 1930 went on to become an outstanding regional organiser. She was jointly responsible for eighty-six constituencies in Durham, Northumberland and Yorkshire for which she received a salary of between £260-£320 a year which was comparable to what she had been paid as headmistress. In February 1930, she formally took up the post which she held with distinction for twenty-seven years until her retirement in 1957.

Margaret joined the party's national staff when morale within the Labour Party was on a high. Labour had formed the Government under Ramsay MacDonald and its supporters had great hopes which by 1931 had been dashed by Britain's recession in the midst of the worldwide slump. The Prime Minister and Chancellor of the Exchequer, Philip Snowden, defected from the Party and formed a National Government. In the ensuing General Election of 1931, Labour saw its MPs fall from 288 to a mere 52.

Even to a professional organiser, the extent of the losses were unexpected and heartbreaking. When the results were coming in from the cities on the evening of Election Day, she recalled reassuring party activists that it would be different the following day,

Oh, wait until you get the mining areas tomorrow. Wait until you get Durham tomorrow, wait until you get Northumberland tomorrow and so forth. Well the picture wasn't any better the next day because we lost everything in Northumberland, every seat. We had two only in the whole of Durham. In Yorkshire, well in total we had seven, so we got five out of Yorkshire. That was the picture…and what did you do next because you hadn't to let yourself get despondent but it was very very difficult. Remember we'd MacDonald in this area and of course there was his triumph in Seaham. (MacDonald had been Labour MP for Seaham and held his seat easily as a National Labour candidate in 1931)….Looking back now, it's still amazing the way the hard core of the party if anything, had just got their determination increased. You felt that something dogged inside people there was no expression of drawing back from what they were doing; it was just, 'we'll damned will come back'.

Like many of the party's organisers she was disappointed by the results in the following General Election of 1935. In her words, 'we expected perhaps too much'. The organisers however, continued with their task of building up the party's strength with considerable advances being made in local government.

The Second World War intervened and it was a further ten years before the next General Election came in 1945. In Margaret's words, the results of the election were accompanied by,

…bewilderment, really and truly. You couldn't believe it. We seemed to win everything… Mind, as time went on, I began to feel we're coming through, but if you'd said to me we were going to have nearly four hundred seats, I think I would have sent you off to some brain specialist.

Now on the night of the closing of the poll on 6 July, a few of us went into the Labour Club in Newcastle. One tough came up and he said, 'He's sent me to ask yee, where are these votes going. Where are all these boxes going tonight?' 'Well', I said, 'They're all sealed up and they're going to police stations. They will stay there until, the three weeks period for the other votes, the incoming

170

forces vote, and then they will be counted'. The response was, 'I wadna believe it'. All that you see, doubts. Someone was going to tamper with the boxes.

Then of course the night when we did get the results coming in, I was back in the Labour Club again where there was never a soul doubting the box. They were all ours, it was gorgeous. I had a flat in Newcastle, my colleague Will Lewcock and a whole lot of us were gathered there and listened to the results on the radio.

Every now and then Will went out to get a newspaper. Now newspapers were all limited so they limited the numbers in each edition. So every two hours, Will would go out and get another and another. He drove up to one newspaper boy, Will never walked if it was possible to move his car. He went to this newspaper boy and the lad looked at him and said, 'No, not to a bloody capitalist'.

Over the fourteen years following the debacle of 1931 and Ramsay MacDonald's betrayal, there had been a steady development of the local parties across the country. In particular, Margaret had seen the potential women could offer. She saw the process of building the women's section as a two-way street. It would help the party but more importantly it offered the women an opportunity to develop their abilities and thus obtain power and influence in the party and their communities. There was an agreement amongst her fellow organisers in the north east region, that she should have a special role in developing the role of women alongside her general work.

Later she explained her approach,

You've got to face the fact that men, the husbands, go out to work. They may argue about football, cricket, what you like, horses but they'll argue and some of them will argue politically. Now that's the man's background, what was the woman's?

By this time she had a vote. It was four walls and a husband coming home at teatime, possibly children coming in and going out. But you see in the thirties it wasn't common, it was uncommon, for a man to take his wife into the club or to take her out for a meal in the evening; in Jarrow quite unknown not quite unknown but almost. So you can see her limitations, not imposed by herself, as against his opportunities. For that reason, it seemed to me that you'd got to do something about the woman voter or she would be left without any real understanding.

Now then, when you got these women together, say there were ten of them, and they'd all be very, very silent in the beginning but somebody says, 'I haven't got one like that' and another woman says, 'Well, you want so and so'. Now they've got off onto something of their experiences. Then if there's another woman there, who's got it about her to say, 'Well you know these are council houses you're talking about, you should get hold of your councillors'. That leads to, 'Why haven't we got a woman councillor?' and in that way you've got women involved.

It seemed to me that we had to do something like that or we're going to lose out. That was why I was always anxious that we should have our meetings where a woman felt she was able to say what she wanted in a way that would get a response. Not just a comment or condemnation and be done with it, but something where they could discuss and take the good points. And you know we got a lot of women on local authorities.

Ever since the Labour Party had created individual membership in 1918, nationally it had placed a great deal of emphasis on the establishment of women's sections. It was also agreed that there should specifically be women's representation on the Party's governing body, the National Executive Committee. It was obvious that political education was necessary as women had the vote but it was also recognised that women had a right to the same opportunities as men. The Labour movement had, from its earliest days, always a number of prominent women propagandists, such as Katherine St John Conway, Isabella Ford and Margaret McArthur and many more.

The extent and effectiveness of women's sections varied from district to district but they were perhaps at their strongest in the North of England. To a large extent this was due initially to Lillian Fenn and then Margaret Gibb; the latter taking them to the peak of their influence.

Margaret Gibb recalled memories in County Durham,

Chester le Street had a magnificent women's organisation. At one time, mind you this period didn't last long, but at one period we had twenty-seven women's sections (in that constituency alone)....Now there, those women put the Labour Party first, everything had to come after, even the chapel. The matter of the chapel came after. It was first and if the Labour Party was going to have anything, well that day was settled, nothing could come.

The Durham miners were magnificent in their support of the women's organisation, always. It didn't matter who were the 'big noises' of the time, they backed the women. Sam Watson was possibly the best. Yes, I think he was the best on the whole.

Whilst the miners gave so much support financially and otherwise, other unions and the men in the party, were also supportive as Margaret was first to admit,

I think they were far-seeing in their way. They could see that there was an awful lot of things to be done in the course of building up the party where the women's contribution could be extremely helpful. I could see, while I was busy, that the more women you can get, who will gather courage to get up and say what they've got to say, not just say it afterwards, the better that is for everybody. So the line I took in meeting the women's groups was, my eye was always on seeing that these women were going to be able to hold their own whether it was men and women mixed or what it was. In addition, they should understand that they had to think out the thing clearly before they got up to say anything.

It was fortunate that many of the local government units in the North of England were rural or urban district councils which were much smaller than the administrations in the larger towns and cities. As a result, many women did not feel as intimidated by them and became effective councillors. They might have been smaller units but they still had a panoply of powers including the provision of housing in which most women had such a great interest. Some very powerful and influential women entered local government through the women's sections.

The importance of being businesslike was always being emphasised by the professional Labour organisers. As Margaret explained,

> We used to stress the fact that if we were going to run the country as a government successfully, we had to do the same thing in our organisation and I was a stickler for time. One of my repeated phrases, I should think anybody in the organisation, would still be ringing in their ears, 'If you say your meetings to start at two, it's to start at two, not five past'. One of my insistent points, and I did try to shape it up into something that was reasonably businesslike, with the result that when the war came and you got all these built-up women's organisations, WVS and all that, whenever you found a Labour woman going in, she jolly well always got a responsible job because she had experience and she had training. That was my defence right through for women's organisation plus the fact that the woman, the average woman, had not had any trade union training. She has today more, but she hadn't then and for that reason she had to have some special care within the party to help to take her rightful place.
>
> I also used to try to enforce my idea that records were important and that a minute book didn't belong to the secretary, it belonged to the organisation and because of that they had a responsibility to look after these things.

She also realised however that it was not sufficient to concentrate solely on business and policy and that many women had other interests,

> I also put it to them that you've got some very good housewives in your organisation but they may not be talkers. I think you should make something for them, as well as for the woman who can argue about India, or Ireland or whatever it might be. So we started a bit of the Women's Institute technique if you like, we started what we called Homecraft Exhibitions and of course, I had a humble start, and it built up and they were quite a feature.
>
> I worked up Cumberland in the same way and I found it did give the woman who hadn't other interests say, 'Oh I always go to Labour Party meetings'. It made her feel she'd got something to

do, even if it was making a teacake, she was getting a place there. Now you call that involvement, nowadays.

Many of the women's sections operated in a very local arena and Margaret Gibb understood that efforts had to be made to try and get these small units to work alongside other sections on a regional basis. Not only could best practices be shared but it would also be good for morale and ensure that the women appreciated they were part of the wider movement of Labour women. She had been one of the founder members of the Durham County Advisory Council in 1923 and saw the benefit of organising initially on a county basis.

Under her guidance, regional weekend and summer schools were organised, excursions were made to other areas and annual galas established. These were held in great esteem by the members of the women's sections right across the region. The various county miners' associations had developed very prestigious annual galas; in Durham's case, 'The Big Meeting' and in Northumberland's, 'The Miners' Picnic'.

At the initial Women's Advisory Council, it was decided to have a Gala along similar lines for the women's sections. The first was held on 9 June 1923, the streets of Durham City were closed with over six thousand women marching with seven bands to listen to Dr Marion Phillips, Jack Lawson MP and Sidney Webb MP in Wharton Park, Durham. It was a magnificent setting, dominated by the Cathedral and the event proved to be a huge triumph. Such was its success that the annual gala became the highlight of the Durham Labour Women's calendar. On 18 June 1927 one was held at Roker Park in Sunderland and then another in South Shields, but the pull of Wharton Park was so strong that it reverted back.

Margaret readily understood the importance and significance of the Gala, and later described its origin more fully,

In 1923, it was decided at a national level that the month of June should be women's month in the Labour Party calendar. It was proposed to help develop the very quickly-growing women's organisation. Durham County Labour Women's Advisory Council backed the idea of a rally to be held in Wharton Park in Durham City. Sections covered the whole County. They were all asked to make a small banner for the procession - white background, the section name in green. We decided to invite fraternal delegates from the Durham County Council, The Federation of Labour Parties, the Durham Miners, Northumberland Labour Women, Cleveland women and every Durham Labour MP (Gibbs, Diamond Jubilee Gala, 1983).

With her new regional responsibilities after 1930, Margaret was enthusiastic to build upon the success of the early annual galas, and explained,

For years, whatever the Durham women did, was invariably bigger than the last year. Now that's an encouraging atmosphere in which to work. They had quite a nationally known Durham Women's Gala. In some cases there were thousands, all carrying their banners. The largest number we ever had was thirteen bands in the procession and we paid for one band, and always the Shakespeare Band, the Durham City Brass Band. All the others were given, either sent from the colliery or paid some money. But we never paid for any bands except the Shakespeare. We had a terrific lot of banners and the press used to go up to seven and ten thousand (attendance).

The 1939 Gala was in June and by this time there was an awful lot of talking of the war. What we did we ordered a terrific lot of white linen and green paint and we made strips and all it had on the white background was the word, 'Peace' in green. All along the procession every section was carrying this peace banner and it was all alike. It was repeated, repeated, repeated the whole line of the procession.

We used to meet in Wharton Park, as you come out of Durham City, and of course it was a magnificent sight. A very lovely Saturday, perfect weather 1947, that was a wonderful summer. They balloted like the miners. A lot of things they did as the miners. They balloted for the speakers and in 1947, they were Aneurin Bevan and Jennie Lee. Well Jennie Lee said they'd made a rule that they would never speak on the same platform but they would come to Durham. (They were a married couple). There was a phrase used in one of the press reports that you couldn't see a blade of grass in the whole talk, and you couldn't. It was just peep-

176

o, peep-o everywhere because of course it was all free. Men and women came in but there were no men in the procession.

It was also the year that there was an Easington Colliery disaster and it had just been, say in the May and we always had our thing at the beginning of June and the Easington Banner, with its little draping of black, was given prominence.

The Northumberland Women's sections were not to be outdone and they had their own Gala which eventually was organised slightly differently,

Northumberland went on with a similar demonstration. It was never as big, all very happy, until 1946. The Northumberland Miners approached us to make a joint effort and we would get our place in their Gala. We get a woman speaker who takes her place on the platform. We've got our place in the procession and everything. That's how Northumberland was worked out.

The Durham Miners gave us the chairman's chain which you'd see the chairman wearing and then of course Northumberland gave their women a chain. They became so heavy they couldn't wear them.

Throughout this period, there was a feeling, rightly or wrongly, that women needed more education if they were to use their vote wisely and to play an effective role as Labour Party members on local councils and in their local communities. Margaret Gibb, perhaps relating back to her training as a teacher, was most enthusiastic in arranging weekend or week-long schools. These were popular with many of the Labour women who not only enjoyed the lectures but also the social side of the schools. In many cases in the early days, it might have been the only leisure they enjoyed in their hard lives supporting their families.

The women's sections usually met fortnightly and were a mixture of the social and educative. They organised whist drives, socials, teas, dances, talks and the like. Occasionally Margaret persuaded them to be more adventurous and include amateur dramatics or musical performances. These began initially in Northumberland but later were also popular in parts of Yorkshire. She was always stressing that the meetings should never get monotonous and initiatives must be followed which stretched the imagination of the women.

> Then we made a feature of trying to get women more determination that they would be heard in the meeting sense. So we did a lot of training. We had some little groups when there'd be a whole lot of subjects in the hat and you had to draw your subject out. You were given five minutes to look at it and then in turn you had to speak perhaps three or five minutes. That kind of thing all meant that perhaps without realising it, they were breaking the ice and in a way it was getting women onto councils, being useful on councils and that sort of thing.

The annual and weekend schools of the 1930s were hugely popular. Money was absolutely crucial, for most of these women had little or no money to spare for such activities. The Durham Women's Advisory Council were well aware of the problem and instituted grants and scholarships to permit these women to attend. Margaret explained,

> They took tests you see and at one time we had tests in different areas. At first we had tests in the Miners' Hall in Durham and after that we thought that it was possibly fairer financially to let the Houghton and South Shields Women have a centre, Jarrow and so forth so there were quite a number of centres. These were just general tests and that went on for quite a long time. Then we let them do it in their own homes and of course I got a lot of criticism for that. People who said 'well people will help do it for them'. Well they may help them but there's no harm in helping anybody and we did it. At the end it was all being done at home and sent in by a certain date.
>
> I sent out a monthly newsletter and, in this monthly newsletter, I always included ten general political questions. The question might be, 'Who was the Prime Minister at the moment?', 'What's his constituency?'; making a question of three bits and that kind of thing. All very simple and then I also recommended books for them to read...I always felt I might touch the imagination of one

or two of them and then after a period when I was pushing books, we sometimes put a question into the test paper.

These tests and the subsequent schools were very professionally and formally run. At a time when the vast majority of women faced severe financial hardship, the bursaries were much in demand.

The schools themselves were heavily over-subscribed. Her predecessor Lillian Fenn had initiated the schools and Margaret Gibb was very keen to build upon her ideas and indeed to expand them. In 1930, Barrow House at Keswick was the venue and twenty-nine women from women's sections in County Durham. It was such a success that the numbers attending in subsequent years more than doubled with venues being in Claughton, Keswick, Matlock, Middleton and Otterburn.

There were always MPs who were prepared to lecture at the schools and they were augmented by other outside speakers. The themes of were always essentially practical, concentrating on training and preparing the women for roles as councillors and other tasks in the movement.

In 1942, the Northern region of the Labour Party gained Cumberland and Westmorland and lost the East and West Ridings of Yorkshire and Margaret moved to Newcastle. But even during the years of the Second World War, the schools continued to flourish as Margaret proudly recounted,

> Well then came the war. What did we do? I think a lot of reading. We could only aim really at maintenance as much as possible. It was no use talking about getting people into the Party and all that.
>
> Then we really just had to go on holding a hard core, doing as much as we could. Of course we weren't allowed to do anything in the way of processions or anything like that but things like schools, I was determined to keep them going as long as I could. There were times when it was a case of trying to find people who would take a fair sized party and there wasn't a school dropped out any-where. We just maintained, we kept our lecturers, we kept our transport. I stuck to the Northern for a long time. I think right through the war. Because of course, once you sort of belonged to these people, you do get consideration.
>
> The schools never stopped, weekends, week schools, they all

went on. A lot of the theme was the future. We used to make jokes about all the people who would be on our boards, our agricultural boards, our marketing boards and all this and I remember one woman getting up and saying, 'well if all these people are going to sit on all these boards, whose going to milk the cows and whose going to grow the potatoes'.

It was a tremendous period of looking forward and the Party produced some very useful proposals for consideration. Now we did an awful lot of that and we also led the way about nursery schools and care of children when more and more women were in employment and that sort of thing. They were much forward looking things and then of course when we got the Butler Act, we had a gorgeous time on that.

So that there was no question of what to do, it was to think what was the most important thing to do and the women responded magnificently. Mind you some women used to say, 'I hope they're all right at home', but we didn't get much of that at all. We were actually in one of these schools when they declared peace. We were over in Dalston Hall (Cumberland) which belonged to the Co-operative Movement and we just more or less had a day off.

We never once missed our yearly schools. We never missed a weekend school. They were maintained right through without any break whatsoever. We took some precautions. I rather laugh at them now but at the time we saw the seriousness of it because I also used to try to enforce my idea that records were important and that a minute book didn't belong to the secretary.

All the Northumberland County records, minute books and treasurers' books and all that went up to Haltwhistle which was a good way from air attack - we hoped. All Durham's stuff went up to Stanhope. The Cleveland area went out somewhere Guisborough way. In the early days, I didn't have Cumberland.

Of course the war came, went, and then you'd see an awful lot of people had been active in the Party, eight, nine nearly ten years, that didn't know what an election was because anything which might have happened in their area was unofficial. We talked about elections. We talked about canvassing. We talked about records. But it was an unreal thing, because they'd never been in on it.

Margaret Gibb, as a trained teacher and former headmistress, knew one key aspect of education and training was never to allow the participants to become bored. It was the responsibility of the teacher and leader to ensure that new ideas and experiences were tried. She accepted this and was never found wanting. In addition to the more routine activities for Party members she introduced others. Lectures by eminent and informed individuals were supplemented by speaking classes for members. 'Any Questions' meetings were held and roundtable conferences were organised whilst other groups were encouraged into plays and shows. She even arranged sports days for the members with local MPs donating the trophies and on occasions Lady Trevelyan presented the silver cups.

All these varied activities had the objective of enhancing the opportunities for the women in particular and advancing the profile of the Labour Party in general. One special activity which captured the interest of the regional press, was the excursions which Margaret organised for the women's sections of the North East of England.

The first and most adventurous took place in the years following the debacle of 1931. In those years, Margaret decided that sufficient recovery had taken place in Durham, that they should take their message further afield. Not to be undersold, she determined on real missionary work by taking the gospel of socialism to the temple of capitalism, Harrogate. In her words,

> You see every penny counted. If you talked about an outing or you talked about anything that incurred personal expenditure, you'd got to talk in sixpences and shillings. I thought out that if Durham women would build up a procession of buses and those buses would go to Harrogate. We would stop at certain points on the way, some buses would distribute literature where houses were on our route. Then when we got to Harrogate we would have a meeting on the Stray. I would arrange lunch somewhere and I would arrange tea somewhere and so forth. The rest of the time they would be free, mind you there wouldn't be much 'rest of the time'.
>
> Well of course the response I got, really shattered me. We had seventy-three buses. Mind some of them were small but in the main, they were the Northern buses, and I had one dreadful fear which I never spoke to anybody. The Northern was of course

solidly trade union and some of the lesser sections were hiring local buses with Tommy Brown and Jimmy Jones running them and there'd be no question of conditions, trade union or anything and I was afraid. However I think, taking an overall look, that those trade unionists on the Northern buses would have said, there's only a few of them it doesn't matter.

Well then we took with us as our guests, and made them work like mad, William Whiteley (former MP for Blaydon) and Josh Ritson (former MP for City of Durham). These two MPs were to speak when we got to the Stray and we were welcomed there by a Yorkshire woman, Mary Bell from Cudworth. She was a character in herself. The only danger with Mary was when she opened out, well she might have been the speaker, because she was always carried away.

Well then the meals were not successful. I don't mean the actual meals but there were too many people. I think the number touched thirteen hundred and I don't think the caterer realised really. I'm not complaining about what he did, it was just overwhelming. What I found was that some of the women who'd lost out on lunch, more or less stood at the door to make sure that they caught up on tea and then of course coming home wasn't as easy because some of them said, 'Well we're on our way home, it doesn't matter' and they persuaded their drivers to do a little bit of slipping. It was an experience but it was bigger than any of us anticipated.

On that occasion, Margaret had been too ambitious and had realised it. However, the thought of thirteen hundred Labour women from Durham, most of them miner's wives with strong north-east accents, descending en masse into the genteel town of Harrogate simply leaves one full of awe and amazement. I'm certain few of the women will ever have forgotten the occasion and it would have remained the talk of their communities for years. But Margaret had learnt her lesson,

Now Northumberland women, they did it one year into Scotland and theirs was much better because it was manageable, that was all. I think there, we had about thirty buses. Well there's a lot of difference between seventy-three and thirty. We went into Scotland and I remember one character telling jokes and in Ashington, saying to me, 'By you're the limit. You make us work like slaves in Northumberland, and not content with that you make us work in Scotland'. Well that was the way she would sum it up you see. It was a very very nice experience and it was a better day because the number was more manageable.

The next year we did it on a smaller scale. I think what we did in Durham was we said, the first twenty-five buses. Then the next year we went to Cumberland, the Durham women did.

Cleveland did a do around Staithes and Whitby where they did a similar thing.

These events had the advantage of allowing the Labour Party to spread its message out from its heartlands but also gave the mainly hard-pressed housewives, the chance to have a coach trip and a day out. These visits became quite established. For example, on 17 June 1933, over seven hundred women from Lancashire and Yorkshire travelled to Kendal on a similar mission and were entertained at the newly acquired Labour Hall. Then the following week, a reciprocal visit took place when Labour women from Westmorland journeyed to Durham and Sunderland (Clark, 2012 p.103). These visits became part of the women's social calendar for the summer months.

Her experiences in the Labour Party stretching from World War I meant that Margaret met all the national leaders of the party. She had firm opinions of, and insights into perhaps the three leading lights, MacDonald, Snowden and Henderson.

The first time I ever was in close contact with MacDonald, no I shouldn't say close contact no, the first time I met him, was in the Smillie by-election (Morpeth in 1923). Now I lived in Dunston and I taught in Crookhill. I used to dash from Crookhill School when the doors opened at four o'clock and went straight to Blyth which was the headquarters for the by-election. Train into Newcastle, then a train out to Blyth and then, though we hadn't many cars, goodness knows, we had very few, I was usually brought to Newcastle at night by car. Then I could get out to Dunston one way or another. Well, this particular night, the Rev. William E Moll, who was a delightful man, and he was a minister in one of the churches up in the West End, he was a terrific admirer of MacDonald who was staying with him. He was doing two nights in Blyth, in the constituency I mean, and on this particular night, they were going to bring me home.

Well, I suppose I was just a member of the Party to MacDonald. He talked but not much, he wasn't very loquacious but I don't know, he did make, he made you admire him. I don't know how and that was my first meeting. Then I remember being at Frognal Lodge (in Hampstead) when we lived in Bedfordshire. We were only sixty miles away and there was a gathering and we were invited, quite a big lot of folk and there was this sale of work. We saw MacDonald there and in the house, in his own house with Ishbel and Alister's wife, it was a nice family setting together. But towards the end we were getting a lot of this Londonderry influence showing and things were getting very taut.

In her capacity as an organiser in the twenties and thirties she came into more regular contact with Arthur Henderson and clearly admired his administrative talents,

Now, I knew Arthur Henderson. We called him 'Uncle Arthur'. He was never 'Uncle' in the friendly sense. I don't know, I think he was 'Uncle' of respect because there's no doubt about it, the contribution that Arthur Henderson made, is immeasurable, absolutely. He was no orator and he was very, at least I thought, very remote. But my goodness, what he did. Sometimes at the time you would think, well that's queer, but afterwards you'd see how right he'd been. A friend of mine tells a gorgeous story of a meeting in Transport House where after the meeting there'd been a definite difference of opinion. I don't know what the issue was between Marion Phillips, the Chief Women's Officer, and 'Uncle Arthur'. Coming along the corridor in a rather silent building, this is what she heard, 'Arthur, you know I'm right'. Then a pause, 'Marion, you're wrong'. A bit further up the corridor, 'Arthur, you know I'm right'. Further along, 'Marion, you're wrong'. 'Alright', she says and he says,

'Alright, you're right'. Those two really basically got on extremely well but there it was you see. Now there was his remoteness, he was sticking to his guns as long as he could. He wasn't a man you could joke with or anything like that. No, he was very much involved in whatever was the issue of the moment he was concentrating on, that he was working out.

Philip Snowden, a Yorkshireman, was for nine years a much respected MP for Colne Valley in the County. However, Margaret Gibb only had dealings with him as a regional officer for two years, including 1931 when he was to leave the Party. She was a regular visitor to the Constituency and would have known the mixed feelings in which he was held after he had deserted the movement. She was very curt in expressing her opinion of Snowden,

> He was more remote still and, mind you, he was terribly protected by Ethel (his wife). She was amazing the way she looked after him, it was simply amazing. But you see if you had a bright idea that you'd just like to go and say hello, you'd have to get past her first. I never had much to do with her. I don't know, I just thought of her as the protector.

In her role of Regional Officer for the North of England, Margaret knew which local political leaders were the 'darlings' of the constituencies and especially the women's sections. In Northumberland in the 1920s and 1930s, they were almost all miners which reinforces the dominance of the mining communities during this period. In particular she singled out,

> I wouldn't say John Cairns, (a miners' leader and MP for Morpeth 1918-23). Ebby Edwards, who was in Parliament, two years, (MP for Morpeth 1929-31), now his standing was exceedingly high with an awful lot of people. Ebby was the miners' leader and then he became national. Another man, in a quieter way in Northumberland, who had a tremendous following of people, who would have gone through life and death for him I think, was William Straker. Oh and another man who died while he was MP,

a terribly popular pacifist, George Warne (Miner and MP for Wansbeck, 1922-28 when he died at forty-seven).

Of course, Sir Charles (Trevelyan. MP for Newcastle Central from 1922-31 and President of Board of Education, 1923-4 and 1929-31) had a big following. Yes, he had a very considerable following. He had the backing, the support, of and was very very friendly with William Straker (General Secretary of Northumberland Miners 1913-35) and with the boilermakers' man, John Hill. He had also a lot of support in the agricultural areas among the forward looking agricultural people. Yes, definitely him.

In Durham, the county in which she was probably most involved professionally during these years, one in every three working men were miners and thus had great influence on the Party. As a recognition of this, she was quite specific,

Now I would say the man in Durham who possibly had the tremendous following, was Jack Lawson (Miner and MP for Chester le Street 1919-50). Jack Lawson was easy, friendly say what you like, he talked broader Durham although he was from Cumberland. Jack Lawson was the most popular MP or public figure.

She spent the late 1920s until 1942 living in Sheffield travelling widely, usually by train, across Yorkshire as a party agent, either in a local or national capacity. Once more she became involved with the women's sections in particular and the West Riding textile districts in general which may have been reflected in her choice of favourites,

Of course you get in that Halifax, Huddersfield, Bradford grouping, I wonder who there was there. In a family way, and a very formidable family, was the Turners, Ben Turner (Wool textile union leader and MP for Batley 1922-24 and 1929-31)). I think that Ben Turner had a definite hold of a lot of people and his family were all at work in the Party, with the result it wasn't only Ben, it was his four daughters. Then, who was the man from Dewsbury, Ben Riley

(Huddersfield councillor in 1904 and MP for Dewsbury 1922-23, 1929-31 and 1935-54). I think he had quite a following.

Now in the coalfield, there was Herbert Smith who was a character, quite a character (President of the Yorkshire Miners' Association, 1906-38; President of MFGB 1922-29). We went into a by-election in Barnsley (1938) when somebody died and our candidate was Frank Collindridge. They very generously said we could more or less have the run of the miners' hall for our various needs and all the rest of it. There was neither a telephone nor typewriter in that whole building. At first, Herbert Smith wasn't going to have a telephone, he'd managed without one for years. However, mind we did, we did get a telephone in but certainly he was a character.

Margaret remained as energetic as ever right to the end of her professional career, constantly coming up with ideas to interest or help Labour Party members in the Region. Even as late as the 1950s, she became conscious that there were still many women who never had a holiday or break. So in 1955, she established the Northern Region Women's Rest Fund run by a committee drawn from three members from each of the regions' advisory committees with the constituent sections being required to pay three pence (3d) per member each year. In the first twenty years or so after the scheme's formation, eight women were sent each year to either Cober Hill Guest House near Scarborough or Mary Macarthur House at Stansted.

In 1957, at the age of sixty-five, Margaret retired but not surprisingly, after a lifetime of professional service to the Labour Party, she simply continued to serve in a voluntary capacity. In 1951, she moved from her Newcastle flat into Cambo Village in the Morpeth Constituency and, within the bounds of her job, became involved in the constituency activities. In her retirement, she was freer to participate but, always ready for a challenge, identified a need to build-up the Berwick Constituency which had continually returned a Conservative MP. Putting her considerable organisational skill to work, she became the General Election agent in 1959 and 1964, before continuing to play a major supporting role in the succeeding elections of 1966, 1970 and the two in 1974 but to no avail. In recognition of her efforts, and of the affection in which she was held, in 1968, she was made the Life President of the Berwick Constituency Labour Party.

Margaret retained her keen interest in life in general and the Labour Party in particular. In spite of the increasingly difficult public transport facilities to and from Cambo, she was always prepared to accept engagements on behalf of the Party. In 1977, she addressed the Annual Gala of the Durham Labour Women's Advisory Council and then in 1983, much to her delight, she attended the sixtieth anniversary of the formation of the Council, being the only founder member present.

She was held in high esteem by the region's MPs and the Northern Group of Labour MPs formally recognised her services to the Labour Party and the Northern region, by honouring her with a dinner and presentation for all her work over half a century. Margaret was always interested in ideas and was an active member of the Tyneside branch of the Fabian Society. Then in 1965, she was awarded an OBE for her services to women in the North East of England.

Margaret Gibb in her later years

She had grown up during those heady days leading up to the new twentieth century, was one of the first beneficiaries of the 1902 Education

Act and thoroughly appreciated the sense of responsibility encouraged by the headmaster at Blaydon School. Her home upbringing was in an all-woman household where, although all the women were professional people, they had no vote. As a teenager, she was attracted by the suffragette arguments. Gradually her interest in wider politics increased and she assumed the radical views of the father she had never known.

However, initially she was attracted to teaching, believing that she could make a real difference in society by imparting knowledge and hope to the children. Her opposition to World War I, which led her into contact with other political activists, made Margaret realise that bigger changes were needed in society. Thus, at the end of the hostilities, she promptly joined both the Labour Party and the ILP, becoming very active in left-wing politics.

Margaret was a gifted teacher and had been appointed as headmistress at the early age of thirty-two. She enjoyed the work and felt it particularly satisfying and worthwhile. However, on the death of her husband in 1927, after a few months break from teaching, Margaret had to make the choice of returning to teaching or moving into organisational work with the Labour Party. She chose to move into the political life full-time and there are generations of individuals, especially women, who had reasons to be grateful that she made that choice.

Having taught for thirteen years in the mining community of Crookhill, she fully understood how hard life was for the miners but also, that it was probably even more miserable for their wives. They were stuck at home and had not even the comradeship of their workmates to alleviate the drudgery. That message remained with her all her life and she continued striving to alleviate that hardship and to offer women, a better life with opportunities and aspirations. It is hard to exaggerate, how much life for so many working-class women was so often changed beyond all recognition by Margaret Gibb's efforts.

Women's sections were important to the Labour Party from the 1920s to the 1990s and especially so in the North of England. Margaret estimated that at their peak, there were over four hundred and eighty women's sections in her region. In 1939 there were one hundred and ninety-six in County Durham alone with in excess of four thousand members.

In these working-class communities, especially during the Twenties and

Thirties, when the North was feeling the full rigours of the world depression, the hope that the women's sections offered to so many women living on the breadline, was massive. Socially, the lives of the women were transformed; the women had experiences other than sheer drudgery and misery. Politically, the women's sections were critical to Labour's support in that they formed the bedrock of the Party's political base for generations to come. The children of the women became the future supporters of Labour. Political socialization ensured that was the case.

Margaret carried across into her political work, the experience and training she had gained as a successful teacher. Her character and personality were such that she had great influence on individuals and instilled a fierce commitment of loyalty and belief amongst her supporters. All this was pursued with great and apparently boundless energy which was accompanied with novel approaches and unending initiatives. She lived up to her maxim that to be successful, one must never appear boring. Life was never dull with her.

Margaret Gibb continued as an enjoyable companion throughout her life. She maintained her avid interest in the political scene and the world around her, retaining always her commitment to socialism as offering a better way to run society. Right to the end, she remained informed, interested and engaged; always concerned about people. Her mind remained lively until her death, following a short illness, in Hexham General Hospital on 27 January 1984 at the age of ninety-one.

Quotations of Margaret Gibb are from interviews with David Clark on 23 March and 17 November 1978.

List of References

Arnot R P, (1953). *The Miners: Years of Struggle*, London, Allen and Unwin.

Calcott M, (1995). *A Pilgrimage of Grace:The Diaries of Ruth Dodds*, Tyne & Wear, Bewick.

Clark D, (1981). *Colne Valley: Radicalism to Socialism*, London, Longman.

Clark D, (1985).*Victor Grayson, Labour's Lost Leader*, London, Quartet.

Clark D, (1992). *We Do Not Want The Earth*, Tyne & Wear, Bewick.

Clark D, (2012). *The Labour Movement in Westmorland*, Kendal, Lensden.

Evans B, Laybourn K, Lancaster J and Haigh B, (eds). (2007). *Sons and Daughters of Labour*, Huddersfield, University of Huddersfield.

Gibb M H, (1983). *The First Durham Women's Gala*, Journal of North East Labour History Society, Vol 17, Tyneside.

Jewkes J and Winterbottom A, (1933). *An Industrial Survey of Cumberland and Furness*, Manchester, University of Manchester.

Jones S, (2013). *Labour and the Suffragettes: An Uneasy Relationship*, Journal of North East Labour History Society, Vol 44, Tyneside.

Jowitt T and Laybourn K, (1992). 'War and Socialism: the Experience of the Bradford ILP 1914-18' in James D, Jowitt T and Laybourn K, (eds). *Centennial History of the Independent Labour Party*, Halifax, Ryburn.

Mann T, (1923). *Memoirs*, London, Macgibbon and Kee.

Ministry of Labour, (1934). *Report of Investigations into the Industrial Conditions in Certain Depressed Areas of West Cumberland and Haltwhistle*, Cmd 4728, London, HMSO.

Nally T, (1939).*The Story of Twenty-one Years*, Manchester, Co-op Press.

Nottinghamshire NUM, (2010). Area History, Internet. http://nottinghamshireminers/Nottingham NUM History.

Pearce C, (2014). *Comrades in Conscience*, London, Francis Boutle.

Tanner D, (nd). *An Introduction to Newport Labour Party Records*, Wakefield, Microform Academic Publications.

Taylor A, (1992). 'Trailed on the tail of a comet: the Yorkshire Miners and the ILP, 1885-1908' in James D, Jowitt T and Laybourn K, (eds) *Centennial History of the Independent Labour Party*, Halifax, Ryburn.

Taylor Lord, (1972). *Uphill All The Way*, London, Sidgwick and Jackson.

Wallhead RC, (nd), *The Keir Hardie Calendar*, Manchester, National Labour Press.

Wheable-Archer W, (2010). *We Really Do Not Alter Just Grow Older*, Yorkshire, CAM.

Williams of Barnburgh Lord, (1965). *Digging For Britain*, London, Hutchinson.

Unpublished

Gibb M H, (1974). Labour in the North Eat Between the Wars.

Gibb M H, (1983). Diamond Jubilee Gala Memory.

Senior H, Woodhead S and Tyas H, (15 October 1927). History of Independent Labour Party (Skelmanthorpe Branch).

Index